Clare Walter.

Working Sheep Dogs

WORKING SHEEP DOGS

Management and Training

John Templeton with Matt Mundell

The Crowood Press

First published in 1988 by
The Crowood Press
Ramsbury, Marlborough
Wiltshire SN8 2HE

British Library Cataloguing in Publication Data

Templeton, John
  Working sheep dogs: management and training
  1. Working dogs – Training
  I. Title   II. Mundell, Matt
  636.7'0886   SF 428.2

  ISBN 1-85223-003-7

Acknowledgements

Line illustrations by Bob Williams.
Photographs courtesy of *Daily Express* (page 12); *Scottish
Farmer* (page 13); Jack Fraser (pages 14, 83); ICI (page 15);
May Templeton (pages 20, 21, 22, 23, 24, 25, 26, 27, 28,
29); *Dumfries and Galloway Standard* (page 85); Matt
Mundell (page 102). All others by Frank Moyes.

Typeset by Acorn Bookwork, Salisbury, Wiltshire
Printed in Great Britain at the University Printing House, Oxford

I would like to dedicate this book to my father and mother for allowing me to get a start in trials in the early days, and for all the encouragement and support given to me. Also to my wife May and family for attending to the work and business at home while I am away. Without this support I am sure my success would have been much more limited.

Contents

About the Author

Just over four decades ago a twelve-year-old Ayrshire lad from a small dairy farm started playing about at nights and weekends with a young black and white collie bitch pup. Two years later he paid 7s. 6d. to enter the bitch, Moss, at his local Sorn sheep dog trials. He came second in the confined section and won £2. It was the beginning of a career on the sheep dog trials fields which has made the name of John Templeton respected throughout the pastoral world.

From those early beginnings shepherding ducks with Moss on his father's farm of Blackbriggs, Mauchline, John tutored himself and his collies to become one of the most consistent and skilled of trainers and handlers with trophies and International Trials appearances to prove it.

John has now won well over two hundred open sheep dog trials and has been Scotland's National Trials champion four times. He won the National Brace Championship seven times and the International Doubles twice. In 1972 over the town moor at Newcastle upon Tyne with the black and white Cap he took the top accolade in the trials world – the coveted supreme championship at the International Trials.

The transition from teaching a young pup on ducks to taking the pastime's greatest honour – and in annually earning the praise and admiration of thousands of watchers at local national and international events – has come purely through following his own self-taught methods of training.

At the back of his mind had always been the desire to produce a collie able to do its everyday sheep and cattle work and, if that extra style and ability was there, to bring it out for trials duties. The seeds were sown when he was given the pup Moss from his Uncle John of South Blairkip, Sorn, in 1946. John was then twelve years old and helped out at nights and weekends on his father's one hundred acre Blackbriggs farm which carried a small dairy herd. The only sheep were hoggs sent from a hill farm to winter at Blackbriggs from November to April.

When John's keenness, aptitude and perseverance with Moss on the ducks was spotted by his father, a score of half-bred gimmers were purchased so that the youngster could have year-round access to sheep. The partnership and confidence between John and Moss grew and in 1948 they entered the confined section at the Sorn trials – an event John has attended every year since, the last twenty-five years in his dual capacity as secretary. That day he came second to the legendary Jock Murray, a handler John was to emulate as supreme International Trials champion.

So the trials career began, when the farm work permitted, and by the end of the 1940s and into the 1950s John was running both Moss and a daughter. The black and white Roy dog was born in 1951, and was running at trials at fourteen months old, purely on vocal commands. John entered Roy and his full

Kway tae me – the author has an unusual method of whistling, using only two fingers of one hand whereas most whistle commands given by sheepmen to their dogs are with one finger from each hand.

brother Hope for the Scottish National Trials in 1955, his first appearance at the event. Both dogs were sired by the Roy dog of West Calder butcher John Purdie. That year Hope brought John his first open victory at one of the country's oldest trials, Carnwath.

Two years later the *Scottish Farmer* got an apt headline out of the butcher's background when John, then aged 22, won the Scottish National Championship for the first time over a course at Dunoon in Argyll with Roy. 'Son of butcher's dog wins', said the paper. In the same year Hope was in the Scottish team and off they went on their initial International Trials foray to Loughborough. Roy was fourth in the qualifying round and supreme championship runner-up to John Holliday and Moss — a mighty performance from someone in his first appearance over the tough course.

Since then John has rarely been out of the Scottish team, and hardly ever out of prize lists at the many open and invitation trials he competes at each year. In 1958 he entered the brace class at the Scottish National for the first time and won it with Roy and Hope. They were second at the International. The next year Roy was third in the singles at the National at Paisley and along with Meg was runner-up in the doubles. When they went on to the International, Roy came fourth in the qualifying competition and, for the second time, was reserve champion in the supreme running.

The next year, after finishing second in the National event at Aberdeen, Roy gained a place in the international team but did not qualify for the final day of supreme class droving. In 1961 the same collie was third in the singles at Stirling but again did not get through the qualifying round at the International Trials.

Roy's daughter Maid then appeared on the trials rounds and at the Golspie Scottish National of 1962 was fourth in the singles. Paired with Roy II they led the doubles. John was the only Scot to qualify for the supreme championship that year at the International at Beaumaris on Anglesey after finishing twelfth in the qualifying rounds. He was third overall. Maid was back the next year accompanied this time by Nap to take the Scottish National doubles crown at Lanark and they went on to become reserve at the York International.

In 1963 the same pair were second in the doubles at the Girvan National — where Maid got into the singles team after coming tenth — and they finished third in the doubles at the International at Drymen. The National was at Inverness the following year and Nap won the Farmers' championship after coming second to John Gilchrist's Shepherds' leader Spot in the overall placings. At the Cardiff International Nap was fifth in the supreme.

Kilmartin in Argyll was the 1966 Scottish National venue and John was runner-up for the second successive year, this time with the Dumfriesshire-bred bitch Shawsholm Fly. Teaming up with Nap, she was also second in the doubles competition. The next year at the Kelso National, Nap had a new partner, Fleet, and they were second in the brace. At the International they gained third place, in a competition held that year beneath Stirling Castle and won by another of the all-time greats, Thomson McKnight's Gael.

John missed out on national team representation for three years before coming second in the National and International

About the Author

Missed by a lot of handlers now is the big Hyde Park international event. This picture from 1965 shows how well Londoners turned out for the contest. John Templeton is fifth from left.

John Templeton won the brace class at the Scottish National of 1972 before going on to win the International Supreme Championship. The Scottish team which went to Newcastle that year is pictured here (left to right) – Jock Murray, Alex Waugh, John Bathgate, Dick Fortune, Willie McConnell, John A. MacLeod, John Campbell, John Kerr, John Templeton, David Shennan, Alastair Mundell, Ivan Young and David McTeir.

About the Author

Scotland's National team of 1980 line up at Thornhill in Dumfriesshire. Left to right – Bob Shennan, Alastair Cutter, Clark Cuthbertson, John Templeton, Stuart Davidson, David McTeir, John Campbell, Sandy Campbell, Alastair Mundell, Hugh McKenzie, William Cormack, Peter Hetherington (judge), George Young (judge), Bobby Cluckie and Geoff Billingham. Kneeling are Ian Stirling, Jean Thomson, Tom Watson and Dougie Lamb.

John Templeton and Roy have a smile for each other after winning the Scottish National Championship at Monymusk in 1985. It was Roy's third win in a row.

Brace Championships in 1970 over courses at Haddington and Kilmartin, commanding Fleet and Cap. The able Cap stepped up for third place in the singles event at the Aberdeen National in 1971 and, along with Fleet, was second in the doubles. At the Cardiff International – where the victor was the man who pipped John in that first-ever confined class run at Sorn, Jock Murray – Cap and Fleet were placed fifth in the doubles.

Cap reached the peak of his performance in 1972, when he was third in the National Trials at Lockerbie and led the brace entries there with Fleet. They then set off for the International at Newcastle upon Tyne where Cap put in the trial's best performance to take the supreme championship crown after coming fifth in the qualifying round.

To make it a rare double for a handler, Cap and Fleet took the doubles title too. There was tragedy early the next year, however, when Fleet died in a motel fire on the east coast of the United States after coming second in the first ever world championship. Like Cap he had been sold to the late Fred Bahnson of North Carolina during that visit, when John and Raymond MacPherson represented Britain in a trial which also had teams from South Africa, Canada and the United States.

John regained his international form when Ben was placed sixth at the Doune National in Perthshire in 1977, but Ben did not manage to qualify for the supreme at the International. Two years later Moss came seventh at the National event and was supreme championship runner-up at the Stranraer International. On Dumfriesshire soil the next year the Irish-bred Max was twelfth at the Thornhill National, and at Bala in North Wales he was third in both the qualifying and supreme courses when the ISDS celebrated its centenary.

John's best ever collie, Roy, appeared in the National team for the first time in 1981. He was second at the Glamis National to his half-brother, Harford Logan's Star, and then went on to be twelfth in the qualifying at the International and third in the supreme championship. Roy gained his first National Championship at Strathaven in Lanarkshire in 1982 and his team-mate Ben joined him to take the brace crown for a great double triumph. Roy finished third that year in the supreme championship at the International held at Blair Atholl.

He repeated his championship victory at national level the following year near Bonchester Bridge where Roy and Ben again topped the doubles triers. In fact, Roy achieved a hat trick that day, also winning the driving championship. When they journeyed that year to the International at gale-swept Aberystwyth, the dogs were second in the doubles and Roy was fifth in both the qualifying and the supreme running.

Over noisy Glasgow parkland at Bellahouston in 1984 Roy and Ben again won the doubles and this time Roy was reserve for the singles. Roy and Ben went on to lead the doubles dogs at the York International. Roy came back to take the third National title of his career at Monymusk in 1985. When the International Trials visited Lockerbie that year he led the qualifiers to win the Farmers' Championship and was second in the supreme. Over the course chosen for the National at Eddleston, Peeblesshire, in 1986 Roy was sixth in the singles and in the International at Beaumaris he was fifth in the qualifying and tenth in the championship.

By 1987 Roy had won nearly seventy trials, one notable victory being the Scottish heat of BBC television's *One Man and his Dog* series in 1983. He also won the Farmers and Driving classes at the 1987 International trials. Since this was written John has won many more trials. The background to his achievements and the quiet, practical, understanding way he has gone about his training of these champions are contained in his own chapters which follow.

Matt Mundell

Introduction

Scotland is the land of livestock – we cherish our reputation and our skill in breeding and rearing livestock which is respected throughout the world. Nearly three quarters of our land is rough grazing which can only be used by sheep and hill cattle, or for forestry.

Perhaps the legendary self-taught poet of the hills James Hogg, the Ettrick Shepherd, summed it up in his much-quoted statement:

Without the shepherd's dog the whole of the open mountainous land in Scotland would not be worth a sixpence. It would require more hands to manage the stock of sheep, gather them in from the hills, force them into houses and folds and drive them to market than the profits of a whole stock would be capable of maintaining.

In other words the sheep dog is irreplaceable. There will always be hill, fell, mountainland and dairy pasture. Men of the world's oldest profession, the stock tenders, and their border collies, will always be needed to tend and improve stock.

The collie must be first, foremost and always a true working dog, an everyday tradesman fit to lift bulk of Blackface or Cheviot sheep from far distances on moor and mountain at the very horizon of whistle reach. Fit too for a day of barking and bawling at the buchts, stells, rees or pens if need be when force and noise is called for to yard sheep for clipping, dipping and dosing, or to heel obstinate bullocks into cattle floats. The ideal dog is one that does all this, then, if his master be sheep dog trials minded, will work just as well on a trials field where canniness and controlled power help sway the judging.

The whole intention at the start of sheep dog trials was to improve the worth of the collies and, perhaps, more importantly, stock farming. Statistics prove the latter but even at a glance, the quality of lamb and beef leaving the heights proves the improvement in farming long before you are down to facts, figures and other things.

Farmers, shepherds and stockhandlers carry much of the credit for the betterment of stock, management and pasture – which is done with the benefit of only a few tools in the livestock sector. The main tool to stock farming, and especially hill sheep farming, is a good hill dog handled well. Like the drench, the vaccine and dip, the dog is one more aid to the hard task of making things pay in the uplands. The trials dog is just a sound everyday working collie which can perform just as well on a jaunt from home as he does on the farm.

As for trials, which we come to later on in the book, they are a test reflecting the everyday environment and tasks faced by the dog – or should be. The trial is *not* a gimmicky, spectator sport. The different phases, such as outrun, lift, fetch, driving, penning and singling and even the gates and the pen, represent geographical features, obstacles and chores which the dog comes up against on his home ground.

We go to trials to see skill, ability and practicality and to hear men, ten minutes of whose company is worth a nightful of television mediocrity. There is nothing of the show-ring about sheep dog trials nor, we hope, will there ever be. The practical man whose dog is needed for everyday purposes does not squabble about colour, shape, ears or tail, though each has his own preference — it is what is in the brain that counts. A border collie capable of winning open trials would not be kept if he could not go out each day and gather sheep or cattle on moor or meadow.

James Hogg tells great stories of his own dogs and those of fellow shepherds — dogs with names like The Tub, Nibble and Chieftain. There are no sophisticated names in the collie world, just plain names which are, in many cases, inspired by the very romance of their environment — for instance, Corrie, Tweed, Mist, Whin, Coon, Glen, Sweep, Shep, Tam, Bill, Roy, Craig, Cap, Spot, Wull, Jean, Nell, Jess, Tess and Fly. They are names which can be shouted quickly and effortlessly through the worst of winter's blizzards and mists high on the bleak slopes and moorland.

The handler's calls to his dog must sometimes leave the townsman wondering if he is in a foreign land. A town dweller must find it difficult to believe *wair-i-me Glen* and *comeinahint Tib* mean *come away to me Glen* and *come in behind Tib*. These are commands which have been handed down through many generations. They are not gimmicks.

There are good sheep dog handlers and bad dogs; and there are good dogs and bad handlers. There are many hill collies good at in-hand work (that is, working close to the buchts and shed-ding and penning the sheep). Others have as their chief attribute what Hogg called 'hirsel-running' — gathering sheep at a distance. Collies will work for nearly three-quarters of the day during lambing time, and I have heard people claim a hill dog can cover over 60 miles on the most rugged terrain on a busy day. It needs a fit and healthy dog to carry out tasks like these and the others which it has to do on its daily trek.

Some shepherds will tell you — others will argue it is impossible — that a good collie can know what heft every sheep belongs to. Other dogs, without a command from their masters, will put a ewe back on its feet if it has 'cowped' (rolled on to its back and been unable to get back on to its feet). Yet others can find sheep caught in bogs, streams and snowdrifts — tales of collies detecting sheep in these wintertime drifts are legendary.

Much of the dog's aptitude comes from initiative, and has to come naturally, but in the major part of this book I will be describing how to go about training the collie for stock work. Training, however, can never be reduced to a system of arbitrary rules. Sometimes people are inclined to try and pressurise too much knowledge into too young a head. Like young children, dogs in their early days have to have their youth and not be saturated with orders, instructions and commands to the detriment of their inborn initiative.

The influence of the border collie has spread world-wide. They have been exported to every pastoral land and in addition to an annual solid demand from the US and Canada, there is an increasing awareness of the role of the collie in Scandinavian countries. Numbers are increasing each year too in European countries such as France, Belgium and

Introduction

Setting off to gather sheep on the hill.

Holland, and trials are now held in several European countries. Exports of collies are probably 50:50 dogs which will be used solely for trials and exhibition work, and those going for their true purpose of everyday stock-tending, at least in the transatlantic deals. Many of the buyers there, a big number of whom come over from the States each year to our National and International Trials, are trial hobbyists with few if any livestock themselves. But I have met many more who take dogs for work on vast mountain and prairie stretches, the type of terrain where stock could hardly be managed without collies. I regularly get phone calls from across the Atlantic from people seeking collies for 'ranching'

— just good hardy dogs that will work commercial cattle and sheep.

The history of sheep dog trials has been well documented, and the coming of trials to television has widened and expanded their popularity. But we have to get on with our everyday work too. Our family have 250 Blackface and cross ewes and 60 ewe hoggs at Airtnoch, which runs to 300 acres rising to nearly 700 feet in an exposed part of Ayrshire. With the imposition of milk quotas our dairy herd of pedigree Ayrshires has been cut back to 90 and we now also have a small pedigree Limousin beef herd. It is a big difference in stock numbers from when we took over Airtnoch in 1965. It then carried 50 dairy cows and 59 ewes.

Feet being pared.

Introduction

Plenty of help here to get the sheep pushed into the pens in the paddock beside the farm.

There is not a day when collies are not used for the sheep and cattle work in a year which, I suppose, begins two weeks before tupping time when the rams are put out with the ewes. From then on (that is about 20 October) there is constant work for both trained dogs and the young collies. We gather the ewes off the hill and drive them into the buchts at the farm where they are dosed with a fluke and worm drench. Their feet are checked and trimmed if necessary. The dogs have a very important role here in forcing the ewes through the penning layout of our buchts.

The ewes are then put on to clean pasture near the farm for flushing, which is the traditional way of ensuring that they reach top condition for mating with the tups, thanks to the better grass. The tups are put out with the ewes on 1 November and the ewes get a little feeding of concentrates during the time they are running with the rams. When the tups are taken from the flocks on 1 January the ewes are shepherded back to the hill. They are given concentrates for another two weeks, and before being returned to the steeper ground they are dosed again for fluke.

The ewes are brought back to be dosed again around 14 February and at this time we have them pregnancy scanned. We have now been doing this for three years and improvements in scanning devices have led to greater accuracy, making the job very beneficial. It means we know how many lambs each ewe is

Young John Templeton dosing sheep in the race.

carrying and can manage them accordingly. Those which are carrying twins are separated from those which will produce only single lambs. The latter ewes are turned back to the hill, where feed blocks containing protein and minerals are made available to them. Ewes carrying twin lambs start to get concentrates after that, starting off with around a quarter of a pound per day, which increases to three quarters of a pound before they start to lamb.

In the middle of March they will be dosed again with a fluke and worm drench. We have to dose for fluke – parasitic flat worms which infest the livers of various animals – as we are in an area of high rainfall. If we did not dose we would have barren and lean ewes at lambing time – if they survived at all –

and some would have little or no milk to feed their lambs. I found this out by hard experience when I came to Airtnoch, for I knew nothing about fluke, having had no problems with it at previous farms.

The ewes on the hill are brought by the dogs into fields closer to the farm on 1 April for the start of the lambing. Once that starts it is a daylight-to-darkness stint for all members of the family – and a variety of dogs. The ewes which give birth to singles are herded quietly back to the hill ground as soon as we find the time to do so once the lambs are a few days old. The twin lambs are moved to another field when they are strong enough to follow their mothers. All the twin lambs are marked with a coloured spray with numbers. This makes it easier to match a lamb to its mother if we find one has got lost – possibly because it was lying sleeping and the mother wandered on grazing with the other lamb. We change the colour of the spray after about 20 pairs have been marked.

Two horse boxes are taken into the fields at lambing time. At nights if we find a newly-born lamb which is not too strong, or if it is stormy, we put it and the mother into the horse box for shelter. It can be a safeguard too against marauding foxes which are increasing with the enlargement of nearby afforestation. Also of benefit at lambing is an automatic twinning machine. This is made of tubular metal with tin sides, and has five sheep-sized stalls. The ewes in their individual stalls face into the centre with their heads restrained so that they cannot turn round and see the lambs. If we have

a ewe with triplets we take one lamb off and by using the machine twin it on to another ewe which has perhaps had a single or even lost her lamb. Usually a ewe will take to her adopted lambs within 48 hours.

All the male lambs are castrated with rubber rings as near to a week old as possible. The lambs get their first worm dose at approximately four weeks old and at monthly intervals thereafter until they are weaned from their mothers in the middle of August. By this time we have also completed the shearing. Our first clip is of yeld ewes, yeld hoggs and the tups early in June. A stock keel mark is put on them before they are walked through the foot trough which contains formalin, and then they go back to the hill. Every farm has a different keel mark

Getting the sheep on the right track down to the farm.

Now it is on with the dipping.

And out comes one very wet ewe.

to identify the farm. Each time we gather the sheep into the buchts — and that now includes two compulsory sheep dips — they walk through the foot trough on the way out. This helps prevent lameness, especially during the summer season.

Our next big job is the milk clipping — shearing the ewes which are nursing lambs. This takes place in the first two weeks of July. The lambs are weaned in the middle of August and cross ewe lambs (about 120 of the Blackface ewes are crossed with the Bluefaced Leicester ram) are sold at Lanark market at the end of August. The wether lambs are put on to good grass and graded through various markets when at the right weight.

We also grow an acreage of rape, a small turnip-like plant, and when the

The ewes waiting to go through the foot trough before returning to the hill.

It's single file through the foot bath – and then back to grazing.

grass is finished the remainder of the unsold lambs go on to this until they reach selling weight. If there is some rape left after all our own lambs are sold we buy in more store lambs to eat off the rape acreage.

The last handling in the sheep year is the drawing of the cast ewes about the beginning of September. We go through all the ewes on the farm and examine their mouths and udders and take out the ones which are unsound. They are put on

to good grass and fattened off for sale from October onwards.

We have boosted our lamb numbers by putting the strongest of our ewe lambs to the ram. In 1987, 50 of these were put to the tup and we had 39 lambs, which is a great boost for lambing numbers. As we are an upland unit rather than a true hill farm the ewe lambs which have nursed their own lambs go on and grow after they are weaned. By tupping time the following

Older ewes are checked to see if their teeth are still sound and they are fit to keep on the farm.

Moving them along to the pens at the farm.

year I can find no difference between these and the hoggs which did not nurse a lamb.

There is little dairy work for the dogs in the winter as the climatic conditions mean we have to get the milking herd into the cattle shed from the end of September. They stay there until the end of April or beginning of May depending on the spring weather. The cattle are in modern loose housing with cubicles and slatted passageways, and are on a self-feed silage regime. In the winter if I am milking the cows myself I take Moss into the shed and he brings the cattle up to the collecting area prior to the cows going into the milking parlour. (Moss is also very keen on loading sheep into lorries for transportation to markets.)

In the summer time the dogs are needed to bring in the dairy herd, as we have them running in three fields. About a third of the Ayrshire herd is bred pure and the remainder plus the heifers are all put to a Limousin bull with the resultant beef calves sold anywhere from a week to six weeks old. Ayrshire heifer calves are kept for replacements. The small Limousin pure-bred herd, which numbers nine females and a bull, was started to subsidise the loss from the dairy quota cut-back.

1 Choosing a Pup

The boffins have tried and failed. They can plot, design, distil, fabricate and manufacture so much for the livestock world: the wheeled machinery, the transportation, the electronic gadgetry, the transplants, the disease resistance, the cures – and the sympathetic bank manager. But they have been unable to produce anything to replace the stockman's most valuable tool: the working collie. It is irreplaceable. Farmers and shepherds, whose daily tasks and very livelihood would be impossible without the sheep dog, are the custodians of a skilled and valued animal which will never find a mechanical successor on hill or lowland pastures.

We have inherited a job and a duty that has been carried on previously by generations of sheepmen and cattle breeders, whose studied breeding policies have honed the collie to be the perfect sheep dog. It is no easy task to continue. There are no short cuts to successful breeding – it can be carefully planned and end in failure; it can be done haphazardly and end in success. It can be carefully planned and succeed; it can be done haphazardly and be a disaster. There are so many permutations, so many individual preferences, fancies and foibles.

This book does not cover all the permutations. It outlines my own thoughts, ideas and experiences beginning with the breeding, selection and choice of pups. The trials successes mentioned in the introduction are the result of over forty years' experience in tutoring, working and trialling collies. My hints come from my experience. They have brought success my way – but there have been mistakes too. I have tried to rectify my own errors and it has always been a case of trying to learn the finer points.

BREEDING

The owner of a good collie bitch has a tremendously valuable asset. But it is difficult to find a foolproof breeding system. The object of planned breeding is to reduce the risk of failure and to try and get the kind of progeny you want. The only point at which the heredity – and the destiny – of progeny is affected is when the bitch is in season. It is essential to keep an in-season bitch isolated as you make arrangements to have her covered by the stud dog of your choice, and to ensure that no other dog gets near.

Stud Dog

The selection of a stud dog will depend on many factors. It is not always the highest prized dog that will be best to put to the bitch. There are many aspects which have to be looked at and carefully researched – appearance, stamina and working performance are among the most important. By performance I mean the dog's prowess, purpose and adaptability at home, in his everyday work or on the trials field, or based on an appraisal of the prospective stud dog's progeny which are already at work. This is perhaps the most important criterion and the one on which the dog must be assessed to find his true value to suit the job you have in mind for his offspring.

It is also worth while to eliminate the shy type of stud dog which has been proved to breed and pass on other faults. The whole object of selection is to reduce the risk of inferior offspring. When looking at and comparing a stud dog's progeny, to consider only one son or daughter is inadequate to prove that a dog (or even a bitch) is a good breeder, as it could be due to a remote chance which might never be repeated. So it is better to assess a number of progeny before making a final choice. The greater the number you see, the more accurate the assessment will be.

A look at a prospective stud dog's pedigree can be of great value, especially if there are names in his ancestry which are of high standing and renowned for their work. The more background information you can find about his parentage and beyond, the better. Equally, it is important to find out faults in the family line, such as lack of power or bad nature. I try and track the pedigrees back as far as I can through the annual stud books of the International Sheep Dog Society.

Right from my early days I studied the work of collies at sheep dog trials.

An example of a collie with good facial expression.

Because I attended a good many during the course of a year I had plenty of time to study particular collies during the trials season. Very often it would not be the prize-winning dogs that I fancied to be mated to my bitches. When I did see a possible stud dog I would go and see him doing everyday work at home.

It is beneficial to know about the home background of collies you are considering as stud dogs, or even if you intend to acquire a pup from someone. Try and see their natural abilities or those of their parents. You can get a fair idea about how natural they are by just knowing their handlers or owners, but I am always keen to see their initiative when doing daily tasks with sheep or cattle.

I like to see plenty of scope about the would-be stud dog, especially on his outrun when going to collect sheep. He must be able to run out well and keep off the sheep, and this must be a natural ability. When I see a fault in a dog at this stage I try and decide whether it is man-made or natural – if it is natural then that is a flaw in the dog I am looking at. I do not mind seeing a dog dropping down on the ground on to his belly if he does not do it too much, and he gets up on to his feet when asked. I prefer my own dogs to go down because they stay there better, as I will explain later. Very often when a dog is standing on his feet he is inclined to take a step or two extra, and when penning sheep or shedding some off from a group this step can put things wrong.

My own preference has always been for black and white smooth-coated dogs when looking for a prospective stud, although I do not mind a little tan colour in them. I prefer the dog to be keen at his work, fairly fast and with a bit of class and power. He must also be a good listener.

Breeding Strain

It was also by watching certain collies at trials that I got a liking for a certain breeding strain. In the 1950s I had seen the late Jimmy Millar's collie Drift and other dogs of the same breeding which impressed me. They were sired by Tam, a black and white smooth-coated dog owned by John Purdie. John never ran at sheep dog trials, but when I saw some sons and daughters of Tam going well I started into that breeding line, as they had good temperament and were fairly strong.

This decision paid off early on in my trials career. In 1957 I won the Scottish National Trials at Dunoon with Roy, who was bred off Purdie's Roy, a son of Tam. Today I still, thankfully, have that strain on the female side of my collies. Though I have continued with the same strain I am not keen, as some sheep dog handlers are, on line breeding or breeding with collies which are too closely related. Line breeding carries the risk of passing on weaknesses, which may take many forms, and will affect the dog's mental and physical abilities.

BITCH AND PUPS

When breeding from your own bitch you should ensure that she is wormed and that injections – for distemper, leptospirosis and parvovirus – are up to date before mating. The bitches should have an annual booster injection, and the best time for these is shortly before mating as the pups will acquire a certain amount of immunity from their mother.

I like bitches to be fairly mature before being lined for the first time. This can mean they will be keener to start back at

Meet the family – a healthy litter of pups in well-bedded accommodation.

their work once the pups have been weaned. A bitch should not be served until she is at least one-and-a-half years old otherwise her growth can be stunted. In the latter stages of pregnancy she should be out having daily exercise and once her litter has been born she should still get some light exercise. I do not have nursing mothers back at work until the pups are weaned at about seven or eight weeks old.

Before weaning, the bitch and her pups are gradually separated for longer spells. Eventually the pups will suckle only once a day prior to their mother being dried off. Even then, however, it will take perhaps a month for the bitch to get hardened into working condition again. Quite a few bitches will have pups twice a year, but the average is usually every seven or eight months. If they are working fairly hard they will not come into season quite as often.

Accommodation

When the bitch is getting to within a week or so of having her litter I let her settle down inside a shed. There are individual pens (around six feet by ten feet) which were originally made for calf rearing and they are always well bedded with

33

straw. The other collies are all tied up inside, even during the summer – when the doors are left open to ensure there is plenty of fresh air.

It is essential to have dry bedding whether collies are kept inside or are in accommodation which has outside runs. If they are outside, the runs should have some shelter for the dog. Sheep dogs do not really mind the cold too much but they prefer to be dry when not working. I have never really liked having collies kennelled outside, as they might be inclined to bark at everything they see. Another major reason is that we are in an area of fairly high rainfall. We get over sixty inches a year so the dogs are healthier inside.

On one of my visits to the United States I was impressed with the kennel arrangements of a friend, the late Fred Bahnson, in North Carolina. The kennels had concrete floors and a wooden bed, raised about twelve inches off the floor, which was bedded with sawdust. Each dog had an individual run outside in a pen with a seven foot high wire mesh perimeter. This allowed the dogs plenty of exercise – something which is essential, especially if dogs are not out working every day. This set-up had a battery of about six or seven kennels in a row. The dogs were able to open a flap themselves to gain access to the outside runs and the whole construction was made to suit differing climatic conditions.

At Airtnoch I make use of existing buildings. When a new cattle cubicle shed was put up a few years ago, I left some of the original cowsheds empty and these are used with collies now occupying the former cow-stalls. They are well bedded in deep sawdust and the collies are let out each day to stretch their legs and have some exercise if they are not

working. I even use the water bowls which were originally in front of the cows. When they are empty I just push the bowl tongues down to give the dogs a supply of water. Wherever collies are kept they should have plenty of fresh water in front of them all the time in clean utensils.

The accommodation at Airtnoch is regularly cleaned out and at least once a year it is steam-cleaned and disinfected.

Feeding

My wife May feeds the dogs a complete diet which is suitable for both the weaned pups and adult dogs. It is moistened with calf milk-powder. The oil in this artificial milk makes it better than cow's milk though, being on a dairy farm, the pups get quite a lot of natural milk carried straight from the cows. Pregnant bitches should always be well fed with a good balanced diet following the manufacturers' instructions. When they are nursing I always feed them to appetite, giving them a meal three times a day. My other collies are fed once daily in the evening after their work is finished.

Health

I always worm the pups at three weeks old and again at six weeks, before regular treatment twice a year after that. At twelve weeks they get their first multi-vaccine injection. These treatments must be carried out under veterinary supervision.

Newly-born pups should be checked to see if they have dew claws. These claws can catch heather and rough grass and will continually bleed if left. They can be quite a hazard. It is quite simple to remove them from pups of a few days old with veterinary supervision, but if left it can be a major operation to get rid of them.

Pups must be kept warm and free of external and internal parasites. I give them a teaspoonful of cod-liver oil once a month to keep them free from rickets and ensure that their coats stay in good order.

BUYING A PUP

Good order and appearance can be a telling factor when buying a pup. Choosing a youngster is quite a gamble; when I choose one it must be from parents registered with the ISDS. I go for a bold pup which comes to me right away, showing no signs of shyness. I find that a naturally bold pup is easier to get on with and will form a team more readily when you start your training.

Appearance

I would choose a pup with a nice broad forehead, high ears, and preferably a black and white coat. But everyone has a different viewpoint and a different liking at this stage. Some say they like the pup which sits back because they feel he is taking notice of everything in front of

Future champions? First impressions of a pup's brightness can influence a buyer and prospective owner.

him. Others choose a pup solely for his appearance.

The expression on his face can be worth a lot – a male pup must always be masculine-looking (usually with stronger bones and wider muzzle) and a bitch genuinely feminine-looking (with finer bones). The Fleet dog which I had in the 1970s looked a bit peculiar with a lot of white markings. As a pup he was definitely strangely coloured and yet he had everything else I was looking for – he was friendly and bold and always first there when I spoke to the pups. So I decided to keep him despite the marks and he turned out to be a very easily trained and able dog – one of the best collies I had for the big events. He was out of my own Maid off my first Roy. Fleet's sire was Weir's Ben going back to J. M. Wilson's legendary Whitehope Cap breeding.

I also like ears to be fairly high set. I do not like loppy ears. There is nothing worse than seeing a dog working nicely, but with his ears hanging down over the face. I do not mind dogs with pricked ears as long as they are fairly high. In a way the Roy dog, which has won the Scottish National Trials three times and has been second and third at International level, goes against that opinion. He has one erect ear and the other is half buckled over. I got him when he was a few months old. He is off my own Moss out of a daughter of the late Dick Fortune's Glen. I just liked the look of him when he was young. He has a small touch of tan but is mostly black and is undoubtedly the best dog I have ever handled and the best listener I have ever known.

Size

When it comes to size I like a medium dog. Big dogs are inclined to be too clumsy. My own dogs are seldom in the house, but it is quite a good idea at a very young age to get them used to different people rather than just their master. I usually try and take a pup about with me when doing jobs around the farmstead. I keep talking to the pup reassuringly, this helps the youngster to get to know his master. You can even detect any faults the pup has at this stage. So when he is weaned get the pup to follow you about as long as he is out of the way of traffic.

ISDS Registration

A final point on the choice of a pup. Potential owners should always ensure that their purchase is from parents registered with the ISDS, who now register many thousands of pups each year.

The Society, based at Bedford with Philip Hendry as able secretary backed by a very capable staff including Dorothy Martin, is the governing body of the sheep dog trials world and keeper of the stud book for the breed. Part of the Society's constitution relates that its main objectives 'shall be to promote and foster within and throughout England and the Channel Islands, Scotland, Wales, Ireland and the Isle of Man, and such other countries as may seem desirable or necessary, the breeding, training and improvement in the interests and for the welfare or benefit of the community of the breeds or strains of sheep dogs, to ensure the better management of stock by improving the shepherd's dog, and to achieve such main object by such as the Society may, from time to time, determine'. This is a very laudable object and

I'm ready. John Templeton's famed Roy – the collie with one pricked
ear and one bent – is poised to start work.

one to which the Society strictly adheres.

The Society adjudicates on many matters for the betterment of the working border collie and these include severe veterinary tests to ensure the eradication, or at least control, of some hereditary diseases which affect the sheep dogs. It is therefore essential to make sure that the parents have passed the strict tests for progressive retinal atrophy (PRA) which is a stipulation before registration. Collies should be tested for this after their second birthday when the defect can be spotted by veterinary surgeons who have undergone special exams before qualifying for panels which do the tests.

Collie eye anomaly (CEA) has recently become a major problem and will feature more in the future. It is a form of tunnel vision in the collie, which can be detected accurately in a pup of between seven and ten weeks of age. I now ensure all my pups are tested at this stage.

Alertness in steering clear of strains with either PRA or CEA will ensure that you are working with breeding lines with which you can progress and have registered.

2 Early Tuition

Sheep dogs are judged and valued on their practical work, whether it is in everyday stock herding or at sheep dog trials. But behind the obvious is the unseen – one of the natural world's great partnerships which depends so much on confidence and temperament. The knitting together of this trust and its subsequent growth begins when you first take the young pup on a daily stroll in the farmstead or around the cottage. So much – more than people believe – hinges on these early ties and so much can be learned by both partners about each other.

The process begins with the pup following at my heels. As soon as I see a pup is able to follow me for short spells I take him out. Usually by then he is two months old, and as he gets older I lengthen the time I have him following me around. I talk to the youngster all the time. This is a crucial start to the partnership that will follow and, hopefully, result in a good working link between owner and animal.

USING A LEAD

A collar is more gentle to begin with than a choke chain, but the pup should not be put on a lead at the outset. I tie the youngster up for brief periods before I start to lead him. This educates the pup to the fact that when he is on a lead he is held.

I use leads which are very light and about three feet long. To begin with the pup simply trails the lead around. Occasionally when the pup passes close to me I speak to him. If he does not respond I put my foot on the lead to draw his attention to the fact that I am there and, because I have said something to him, I expect him to listen.

I keep to this routine for a week or so as time and duties permit. Sometimes I even go out at nights to the shed where the youngster stays and put him on the lead. When on the lead he should learn to walk properly and just slightly behind me. A trainer should always act gently with a pup. He should not be frightened of his master at this stage, or at any time in training. When talking to him I show some affection if he is doing the job properly. This also helps the pup to gain self-confidence as the partnership steadily grows.

FIRST COMMANDS

I do not hurry into new things. The pup has to have time to think for himself, and I will willingly spend a lot of time on what might seem to be small phases of the early tuition.

Lie Down

My method to get the pup to lie down is to place the lead under my foot and push the youngster down to the ground with my hand at the same time, giving the

Teaching the youngster to lead properly just behind the trainer.

A foot on the lead will keep the dog under control at an early stage in the training.

Pushing the pup to the ground to teach him the *lie down* command.

command *lie down*, followed by a low, short whistle. This will be the only whistle order I will use until the pup is fairly well on in his training.

The pup should be held down for only a few seconds at a time. I always straighten up each time after pushing the pup down, which should give him the impression he is more or less doing it on his own. I keep the lead fairly tight with my foot but do not persevere too long before starting the same procedure all over again.

Get Up

Once I am sure the pup is going to remain in position when I ground him, I tutor him to get up again. I keep the lead tight under my foot until I give him the command *get up*.

These lessons are repeated regularly, but not necessarily every day as this gives the pup a little time to think about the performance. Until the young dog will perform these moves correctly I will not go any further with tuition. This can take quite a few days and in some cases it can extend into weeks, so do not give up.

My old Nap dog was one which came into the latter category. I bred Nap

Making sure the pup stays after he is ordered down.

myself out of my Maid put to the late David Moodie's Nap. As a youngster Nap was a natural dog as far as standing on his feet was concerned, but he just did not want to lie down when I started to train him. In fact he hated it – he would wriggle and try to get back on his feet and this went on for long and weary weeks. He was the only collie I trained on which I had to use a choke chain. I really had to be firm with him, giving a short sharp tug with the lead and putting him back down gently. Finally he realised I meant business and gave in.

Slipping the Lead

The next stage in my training programme is to drop the lead and let the pup trail it again. The youngster now has the feeling that he is still being held and he is inclined to obey and pay more attention to my commands. It also means that the pup is easier to catch and correct if he disobeys.

After some spells practising and making sure the pup is doing the correct moves I slip the lead – preferably one with a snap hook – off the collar. The idea of the snap hook is to prevent a tussle with the pup when undoing it which would take away his concentration.

By this stage I am usually confident the pup is going to respond to my commands. If he does not, then for the first two or three times off the lead I keep him in the shed so he cannot get out of my reach.

That'll Dae

The pup also has to learn to come to me when I command him with the *that'll dae* order, which is one universally recognised in the sheep dog world though given in different dialects and, of course, meaning *that will do*. As I give this command I slap my leg. When the pup goes out of the shed with me round the farmstead I hope and expect that he will by this time be listening to everything I say and will also be watching every move I make.

I like the pup at this stage to come smartly and freely to me when I ask. If he does not, I will work on this problem and may even encourage him with a small snack to get him to come to me faster – and enjoy coming to me. The pups will follow me individually at any daily work I am doing around the farm. We are lucky at Airtnoch in not having a public road nearby, but it is very important that those who live near highways should be aware of the potential danger.

Building up Confidence

Building up the pup's confidence is of premier importance – and also making sure that he is listening to what you are telling him. This makes the job an awful lot easier when you eventually take the youngster to sheep.

Discipline

When teaching the pup early commands it is essential to do so in brief spells. Most of the dogs I have had, except Nap, accepted them quickly enough. If at any time there is a sign of disobedience, I give the youngster a sharp tug on the lead and at the same time give the command again in a stronger voice.

I never put any more commands on him than is absolutely necessary, but there has to be a firmness with discipline right from the start.

The young dog gets some praise after a teaching session is finished.

The Pup and Livestock

It is very difficult to know at what stage you can gauge whether or not a pup is going to be a working dog. But when you see him eyeing hens or stock in courts you can sometimes get a good idea.

When I am feeding cattle inside sheds I take the pup with me, although he is not, of course, allowed in the courts or pens. This often gives him his first sight of cattle, and he will be alert, looking at the cattle or calves through the penning, watching what is going on.

He will also, by this age (which can be anything from six months to a year old), have spotted the hens in the yard and, hopefully, have shown an interest. At Airtnoch the hens are the only livestock moving about the yard, and so most pups will start keenly watching them. I pay quite a bit of attention to the pup when I see him watching the hens, as this gives me some idea of when he will be ready to start on stock. It is quite useful for the pup to experience animals at close quarters before you introduce him to sheep, and I believe that if a pup does start to work on hens you can put a little command on him. The first collie I ever trained started working on ducks.

My young dogs can be nine or ten months old before they even see sheep. I do not usually push them until they are big enough and old enough to go past sheep and have a bit of speed in them. Occasionally, I will lead them to see sheep, but until I see they are ready, they will not be taken off the lead.

Cars or Tractors

I have seen young dogs which showed eye at a passing tractor, and not so long ago I had one which did the same with cats. It is just a natural instinct to work anything which moves. The one thing to discourage is the pup which does eye cars or tractors. So often I have heard of a dog which has been killed by a tractor or car being described as 'a beggar for going for tyres'.

There are many farm dogs which are inclined to chase cars or thunder across farmyards chasing planes or birds. Keeping the dogs inside a shed can prevent this, for it is often because a pup is lying idly outside that he picks up these habits.

Feeding

At this stage, following weaning, the pups are being fed twice a day and this will continue up until they are about six or seven months old. A lot depends on how they are growing – if I think one needs a little extra then he will get additional feeding or the twice a day meals will be continued longer.

3 Seeing Sheep

The handler's eye and the collie 'eye' are two of the most important factors when a pup is introduced to sheep. Having carefully watched the young dog in the yard you will have seen if he takes notice of anything that moves – showing eye by stalking hens or ducks or even walking up to penned cattle.

When a collie shows this eye he is wearing or stalking livestock. He walks in a set position with his head slightly lowered, his back end a little higher and with his tail nicely tucked in between his hind legs. I do not like to see the tail right through below the dog's carriage. This indicates quite a bit of tension or a highly strung or nervous dog which can be very difficult to deal with, especially in the early stages of training.

NERVOUS DISPOSITION

It can take many extra sessions to try and conquer a pup's nervous disposition, which may never completely disappear. It needs perseverence and patience. Careful tuition and management, however, should improve the situation.

I have only had one really nervous pup myself. He was out of Bet, a daughter of Millar's Drift and my own Moss bitch. The sire of the pup was Whitehope Nap. He was only really shy in the company of other humans. He was fine when with myself and other members of the family he knew, but when a stranger appeared he would slink off and stay at a safe distance.

Not having come across this problem before I was at a bit of a loss as to how to deal with it. He was a good sort of dog and a nice looking one, and I desperately wanted to try and improve on his nervous disposition.

One day when our veterinary surgeon, the late David Moodie, was at the farm and had finished attending a sick cow he asked me what the young dog situation was. David was always interested in sheep dogs and had bred and run collies himself at trials. I told him about the Whitehope Nap pup and his shyness with strangers, and he asked if he could see the pup working. David was standing in the doorway of the building when I went in to let the pup out. It shot past him as though fired from a gun.

We went down to the field where hoggs were being wintered, but the pup would come no nearer than twenty or thirty yards behind us. I told David to stand there and I went on, calling Nap up to me with no trouble at all. I then let David see the pup go through his paces, but occasionally he would look back at the stranger. When I had finished work, David came closer to the sheep and the pup started to go away. There was no way I could get him near when David was close to the sheep.

On the way back to the farm we were discussing what would help to sort out the pup's nerves, and David suggested he take the pup back with him to his home in Ayr. Each morning David walked from his house to a shop for the newspapers. One of his philosophies was that if he took the pup with him among the early morning workers and shoppers on the pavements this would get the animal to understand he was safe with other people.

David had the pup for about six weeks and when he came back he was a completely different dog. Although I did not have enough confidence in him to compete at sheep dog trials he turned into a really first-class working dog, and when I sold him to a hill farmer he remained there until he died.

FIRST MEETINGS

A pup should be mature enough to go round sheep before he is taken to stock for the first time. At home I have the snap hook on his collar and lead him. I always take a trained dog to cover and steady the sheep in front of him. I usually use Blackface hoggs for the first lessons and I get the older dog to bring them as close as I can to myself and the pup, keeping the youngster on the lead until I see what his first reaction is going to be. While still on the lead I give him all the various commands he has already been taught in the yard – *lie down*, *get up* and *that'll dae* – and I walk him round, following the sheep while keeping control of these with the older collie.

It is very important to have a broken dog which responds to light and quiet whistle commands in the background without the pup knowing about it. In fact, if he is concentrating and studying the sheep the youngster will not hear these commands to the controlling collie. The general idea is to move the sheep

yourself, giving the pup the impression he is doing the job himself. I just walk around in any direction – it does not really matter where the sheep go. I keep ordering the pup to lie down and then get up. When the pup gets to the end of the small lead I stop him and give him the *lie down* command, making sure he obeys.

My Roy and Ben dogs are ideal for helping to tutor a youngster by controlling the hoggs. They stay where I put them and never move until I tell them. It is not necessary to have quiet, docile sheep while you are steadying them with a trained dog. In fact, the more movement with the sheep the better chance you have to study the reactions of the pup.

If a trained dog is not available when introducing a pup to sheep for the first time, I always put the sheep in the stackyard. This is usually a small fenced or dyked enclosure on farms, where in days gone by the farmers and crofters built their corn stacks after the sheaves were carted from the fields, awaiting the winter visit of the travelling threshing mills. My own stackyard is roughly quarter of an acre or so in size. The sheep cannot, therefore, get far away when I am trying to get a pup started.

One instance of how a sheep dog trainer made use of existing features happened when one of the lads I was tutoring at an Agricultural Training Board course on work dog training said he had no stackyard or small field. The only enclosure was a sixty-acre fenced block on a thousand acres of rough hill land. So he made use of the biggest handling pen he had – one of the buchts. After I introduced him to this method he got started with a young dog and progressed very quickly.

Nowadays many progressive farmers have large custom-built sheds for inwintering sheep. They are often empty for a good part of the year and they can be used very successfully for the first stages of starting off young dogs. They are also a lot more comfortable in bad weather for both trainer and dog. I am sure that I am not the only one whose patience and temper last a little longer if I am under cover, so these big sheds are an advantage.

All this is a far cry from the conditions I worked in when I tutored my own first pup, a little bitch called Moss. I was still at school, travelling every day from my father's farm at Blackbriggs, Mauchline. It was a small dairy farm milking thirty cows. There were no sheep at all except some wintering hoggs which usually came at the start of October and went away on 1 April. But we did have twenty ducks. Little Moss started herding these ducks on her own, walking behind them and wearing them into every corner of the farm. I had acquired Moss from my uncle, also John J. Templeton, who was on the neigbouring farm of South Blairkip. Her mother, my uncle's Jess, was by the famous war-time breeding dog, J. M. Wilson's Cap. Moss's sire was a son of Tom Bonella's Spot, one of the better dogs of the day.

She was eight weeks old when I got her and I remember, when watching the local Sorn sheep dog trials with my uncle (the first I ever attended), I decided I would run Moss the following year. Watching the trials that day, however, made me realise just how many complications I was going to face, so I had a rethink about my ambitions for the following year, and gave myself a little more time. I returned to working young Moss with the ducks, under protest from

my mother who always claimed the poor birds would not lay any more eggs because of the chasing they endured. But I persevered with Moss and eventually achieved great success with her.

INITIAL REACTIONS

When introducing the pups to sheep, it really does not matter how you approach the stock. The point is to make sure they get a bit of action. If they try their best to get to the sheep or wear them or show a bit of eye then you will know they have the potential to be good work dogs. If, however, they do not show any reaction at all I usually just let them off the lead and keep working the sheep around with the other dog, keeping the pup near me. This is the only time I really work the older dog while the pup is working.

So far, every pup I have had has taken to his tuition in time. Most of those which have tended to work stock in the yard will do the same when they go to sheep. Nap, as I have said, was a beggar to train when I first introduced him to sheep. He wanted to be at them all the time and was on the lead for longer than the average pup. I had to lengthen the lead to about thirty yards before I could let him off. You just have to watch their reaction continually, especially the first time you take them to sheep. This will tell you how long you can expect them to remain on the lead.

Every pup makes a different approach at first. Some pups look frightened and scared and cower back when they first see sheep. You just have to take a little more time and coax them nearer the sheep, reassuring them that they are safe and will not be attacked by the ewes or hoggs. My own Fleet was like that. He would work away fine with cattle but when he initially saw sheep he was quite frightened.

Keeping them on the lead for a little bit longer will also stop them from running back to the shed, which is a habit that can be picked up quite quickly. If they are sensible after two or three sessions you will be able to let them off in an enclosed area, preferably this time with quiet sheep.

An example of how a young pup can acquire a real interest can be judged from a six-month-old one I had last year at Airtnoch. I took him with me in the farm pick-up when feeding ewes prior to lambing. When I was putting the feed in the troughs I had him tied to the tow-bar and he watched closely and showed a bit of eye. So there are several ways of getting them accustomed to sheep.

Lambing time, however, is not a season when young pups should be near ewes. They could perhaps get a bad bump from a maternal ewe which could knock confidence out of them for a while. They can also be a nuisance when you are busy and do not really have the time to give them the right amount of attention.

I do not pay an awful lot of attention to pups which try to, or succeed in, gripping a ewe and its wool at this stage. I do, however, try and prevent it as quickly as possible and stop the possibility of the youngster acquiring the habit, but as long as the grip is not too severe I am not unduly worried. A reprimand should be all that is needed. I find that gripping is an easy thing to halt.

4 Come By

INDIVIDUAL TRAINING

Each pup is different. Each has a distinct personality, which will be especially noticeable when the youngster is taken out for the first time to see and work sheep. Each one, therefore, requires a subtle deviation from standard procedures in training. So the pup's reaction to the first sight of sheep has to be carefully studied before he is let off the lead near the stock, which should still be held steadily in position by an experienced collie.

Once the pup is off the lead you have to make up your mind how the job is to be tackled. Personally I do not mind what the pup does when I release him. As long as he does *something* I know I can finish up with a working dog or bitch. Some pups will lie down and stare at the sheep. Some will go all out to get at them, and others will stalk them, walking after them all over the field.

The Hesitant Pup

So how do we go about training the different types? If the pup is one which lies down and looks, I will go round the sheep myself and put the trained dog round to where the pup is lying. I make him move the sheep away from the pup using whistles on the experienced dog and talking to the pup, giving him the *get up* command. The pup can be so engrossed in looking at the sheep that he may never hear me and will not take the command as he did when getting his earlier tuition in the yard, where he only had me for company and there was nothing else to take up his attention.

On the other hand he might get up and follow the sheep. That is a good start. If he does go behind the sheep I walk backwards trying to balance the sheep between the pup and myself, keeping the pup, the sheep and myself in a straight line. I will be doing the dog's job for the time being. I stop the pup occasionally and then ask him to go on again, but I always have the trained dog in the background to assist if necessary.

If I have any trouble getting this type of pup to go forwards I put a long light lead on the collar, which can be anything up to thirty feet long. I can then give a sharp tug on the lead while talking to the pup to draw his attention to the fact that he has to listen to me whether he is in the yard or out at the sheep.

The Enthusiastic Pup

Then there is the type of pup which will go all out to get at the sheep, sciff closely past them or even go through the middle of the group. I admit that I like to work with this type because I know I am going to finish up with a really good work dog and, possibly at the end of the day, with a trials collie. When I am training I have at the back of my mind what the standard of the finished work dog will be because there will always be a demand for a well-trained, practical dog.

The pup, the sheep and the handler should be in a straight line.

The type I have just described is no more difficult to train than the first one. It just requires a different technique and different approach: instead of getting his attention to go forwards I have to get his attention to stop. When he is trying to get at the sheep – and the ewes or hoggs in these early training days should always be in the middle of the field where there are no obstructions – I go all out to stop him. This is where the trained dog comes in handy to keep the sheep in one group and as near me as possible.

If I get the chance I try and step in front of the pup, holding up my stick and hand to attract him to the fact that I want him to do what I am telling him – just the same as he was doing when he was slightly younger, in the yard or shed.

The Nap dog I ran in the middle 1960s with some success at trials was very much this type of pup. I had to put a cord of about thirty feet or longer on him. I let him trail this and when he got unruly I put my foot on it and gave him a verbal ticking off at the same time for a few sessions, just to keep control of him.

The Stalker

The third type of pup, which will stalk sheep, can at times be very frustrating to say the least. It can be a long slow procedure to get them going properly, and they require a lot more patience and perseverance. This kind usually stay on their feet and are unlikely to go to ground. Dogs which stalk are also inclined to raise their tails, but this habit disappears once they are more advanced in their training.

The Maid bitch I ran at trials in the late 1950s was a bit like this. I could get her to go round so far in front of me but when I stopped, she stopped. Then I would do the same on the other side. I went on like this for a while getting her further and further round until I started going the opposite way from her, trying to get Maid, the sheep and myself in a straight line. Suddenly it clicked with her – she realised she had to be at the opposite side of the sheep from me.

That very first Moss bitch I had which began her training on ducks was similar in her early days. At that time I thought it was my inexperience which was preventing us from getting on, but in fact quite a lot of pups start this way.

I am inclined to work with this type for shorter sessions than usual. One aim is to try and excite them and get them to speed up and pass the sheep, so I move the sheep about quickly with the trained dog. This faster movement of the stock will do the trick eventually along with a bit of hissing and hand-clapping, which gives extra encouragement if the pups are concentrating too much on the sheep.

This power of concentration is called 'eye' – a strong-eyed dog is one with too much eye. These collies are usually very classy and move in a frozen position, never taking their eyes off the sheep and concentrating too much on their charges. They are not listening to what they are told. They are very hard to flank about because their eye is constantly on the sheep. They will also approach the stock in a rather cautious manner which makes them look weak.

On the other hand, if a dog does not have enough eye he will have no balancing point on the sheep. Such dogs are inclined to be very plain with head high. The opposite of the strong-eyed dogs, they rumble about, approaching sheep too quickly and scattering them. So we are looking for a happy medium between the two: a dog with a nice posture when

A collie showing the power of its eye, this time with calves.

walking, and one which is easily moved about.

IMPORTANT COMMANDS

When I introduce pups to sheep I want to see them listening and obeying, so I do not really bother about what kind of work they are doing at that stage. I then proceed to put the 'sides' on them — that is, getting them to go to the back of the sheep either on the left or right-hand route. The *come by* command orders the dog round in a clockwise direction. Standing in front of the group of sheep, I make the pup stand or sit at my left side

and try to make him look at the sheep. I take a slight step forwards in front of him and call *come by* together with his name and let him go to the back of the bunch of sheep where I order him down with the command to sit. Then I give him the command to get up and move the sheep only a short distance.

The pup is then called back to me with the *that'll dae* call. After or along with each command, the dog's name must be given. Initially, to get him to return to me with the *that'll dae* command, I usually go to the side of him and attract his attention. I may have to lean down sometimes and say *that'll dae*, and if he is not paying attention walk to the front of him and try and keep between him

Stepping in front of the dog to give it the *come by* or *kway tae me* command (in this case it is *kway tae me*). The dog's back should be to the handler. A hiss to the dog will indicate he has to look for sheep.

and the sheep to do so.

I repeat the exercise on the other side, sending the dog in an anticlockwise direction. The universal command for this is *come away to me*, but to avoid confusing the dog by starting off with the word *come* which he might associate with the *come by* call, I shorten or Scotticise the anticlockwise order to *kway tae me*.

At this stage when the pup is behaving correctly I give him some praise and if he is keen and willing I will repeat the exercise on both sides. I always walk back each time bringing the sheep with the dog a short distance to make him think it is he who is gathering them. I may work

on this aspect for about fifteen to twenty minutes and if I see any sign of boredom or lack of concentration I immediately stop – again with some praise. While we walk back to the farm I allow the pup to run and play with the other dog to make him realise his duties for the day are over.

CONTROL OF THE SHEEP

At the time the pups are learning how to gather the sheep, the older dog can be anywhere in the background. If the youngsters are keen to work they will

Come By

Sending the dog clockwise is the *come by* side, while anticlockwise is *kway tae me*.

Clapping a hand on the trouser leg after giving the *that'll dae* command
to call the dog off the sheep back to the trainer.

seldom look at the other dog. If they do, however, I immediately put them into a smaller area where I can keep control of the sheep myself and put the older dog in the house – although this very seldom happens. The important point to remember is that you do not want a young dog to be dependent on another one.

At this stage in the tuition I usually have eight or ten sheep for the pup to work. This size of flock can be moved more easily. If there are too many sheep – say fifty or sixty – they might spread out too far, sending the pup further out of reach and possibly making him come through the centre of the group. A group of only eight or ten sheep will usually stay bunched together and not be inclined to break into small packets.

I always try and use sheep which are used to collies, often using a few hoggs I keep closer to the farm to help put polish on the experienced dogs prior to trials. But at certain times of the year it can be yeld ewes. I do not recommend rams for they may be inclined to charge at a pup.

SOME COMMON FAULTS

I stay as close to the sheep as possible when tutoring the pup to get him started, and keep the run out to get behind the stock very short. Even at this stage you can get an idea of the youngster's potential class and see if he has power. You will also be able to tell if he has perhaps too much or too little eye. If the pup is too strong in the eye I try and hustle him on a bit.

If a young collie keeps looking back at you, this is a fault, which means he is not keen enough and not quite ready. In such a case it is better just to leave off for a while until he matures further.

Should the pup be a bit slow in taking up commands, you just have to persevere until he understands the different orders.

If sheep break out of a group it is better to put the pup on a lead until you have control of them again. But if there is a good trained dog near at hand this should not happen.

Making sure a pup stops when told is of premier importance. If you cannot stop him you cannot get him to take the next command.

Do not spend too long at this training stage for the one thing you do not want is boredom in the pup. It is probably best when introducing them to sheep to work for two short periods a day rather than one long session.

5 Collie in Command

FLANKING COMMANDS

Once the pup is able to control the sheep at close quarters he is ready to learn how to go round the stock and gather them. He can now be taught to accept the flanking commands – his moves to the left or right as required, in order to keep the sheep in a straight line or to move him to the position where I need him. Initially, while the dog is learning to gather, there will be approximately thirty yards between myself and the sheep.

The first step is to put him round the sheep, stop him, then move him up to the stock. I walk backwards a few yards and then stop the dog, giving him the *lie down* command. I move to the side of the sheep and let them drift past me. When they have gone a few yards past me, and if the dog is on my left, I say *come by* and step forwards to ensure he goes the way I am telling him, and to encourage him to go right round to the point of balance. That is the point where he will finally stop the sheep.

I stop him there and bring him up to the sheep, again moving the animals towards me while I walk backwards a short distance. This time I move to the other side of the sheep and let them slip past me on the opposite side. I then give the command *kway tae me*, and step forwards to make sure the dog takes the

right command and goes in the correct direction. To finish the exercise, do the same as I did on the 'come by' flank – put him right round to the point of balance.

I repeat these right and left commands for a few weeks, gradually lengthening the distance between myself and the sheep. However, it is important to ensure that the dog does not go too far and make mistakes. If the sheep drift off to one side I give the *come by* or *kway tae me* commands to straighten them up again.

FLANKING DISTANCE

At this stage the different behavioural patterns in pups will also be apparent. Some pups will instinctively run round the sheep at a nice distance, just wide enough not to disturb the sheep. I find this type quick to train, but I have also found them just a little weak. Often more time is needed to bring them closer to the sheep and to get them to come quicker to lift the stock. This can be done by giving the pup plenty of encouragement and praise and by exciting him slightly.

When I think of this aspect of training I recall a bitch I once ran, Shawsholm Fly. She was half trained when I bought her and it was very difficult to put her off her natural curve round the sheep. If I wanted her further out than she was, I

In tutoring for the gather, move to the side of the sheep, let them drift
past a few yards and then ask the collie to *come by*.

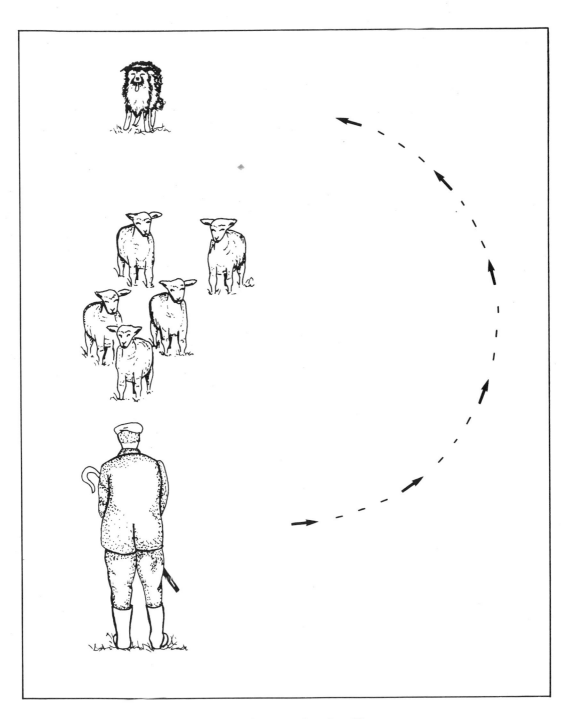

Encourage the dog to the point of balance – the point where he will stop
the sheep.

The older dog (left) has steadied the sheep and the young collie is on the
come by flank going to the point of balance behind the sheep.

had to force her out. When I wanted her
to come further in on the flank I had to
coax her very gently, stopping her on the
flank, bringing her up to the sheep, flanking her a little further round, stopping
her there and bringing her in again. After
a whole winter of tutoring, I could bring
her in or out and flank as I wanted.

Too Close

A young dog that is inclined to be too
tight when he starts gathering is perhaps
easier to teach – he is close to the sheep
when I want him, but will have to be
taught to move further out. I do this by
keeping the sheep as close to me as possible and getting between the stock and

the dog, ordering him further out all the
time.

If this fails and he is really desperate to
get in close, when the sheep are near I
put him round them on his flank command (either *come by* or *kway tae me*)
and go right through the centre of the
sheep myself. If I can reach the back of
the bunch at the same time the dog
arrives, I can then order him further out
giving a definite command to get back.

I usually put this type of dog further
out on his flanks than he really needs to
be because such a dog tends to be
strong-willed and is therefore very easily
brought back in. It is essential to be
completely in command of this type of
dog as he will disturb the flock if he does

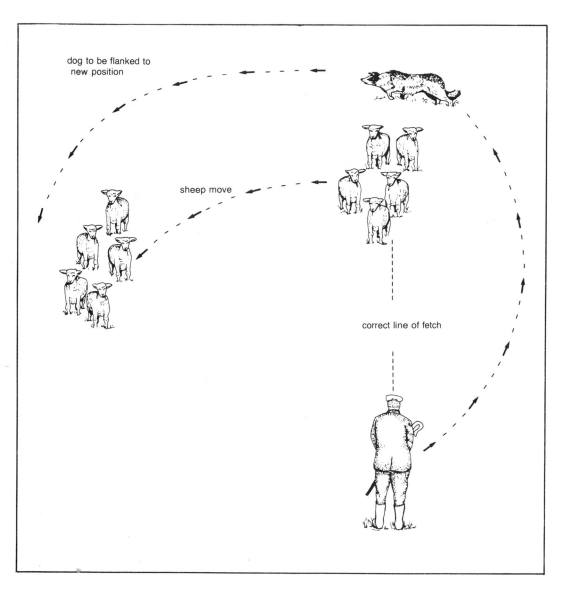

dog to be flanked to
new position

sheep move

correct line of fetch

If the sheep drift off give the collie the *come by* or *kway tae me*
command to cover them and bring them back on line.

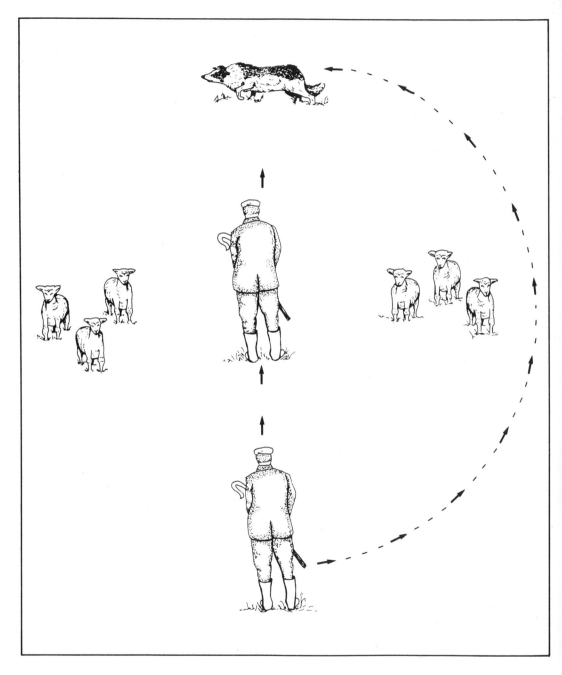

To make sure the dog keeps off the sheep I would ward him out by
going through the centre of the sheep myself.

not run wide enough. This will be particularly important when the dog comes to work with in-lamb ewes, which must be done gently, quietly and with a minimum of disturbance.

When putting a young dog out wider on his flanks the trainer must be very careful not to overdo it as the young dog can get it into his head that it is wrong to be in too close to the sheep at any time. This may spoil the dog, and his re-education can take a long time. I have done this myself on more than one occasion. It is very easy to overdo it, especially if the temperament of the young collie is not just one hundred per cent.

Too Wide

I find the most difficult type of dog to train is the one that wants to be too wide. This type can be quite a problem as it will run too wide to work the sheep properly. The tendency to run wide may indicate a weak character, and is a bad fault in that the dog will approach the stock very slowly, giving them time to react.

I tackle this type of dog in a very small area, such as a tiny field, the stackyard or even in the shed or the buchts, where he cannot back away from the sheep. I keep flanking him back and forwards one way then the other between the fence or wall

The dog squeezing between the fence and sheep during training to keep him from going too wide.

and the sheep, holding the sheep fairly close to the fence with a trained dog, and keeping the youngster on commands and movements he knows. These are usually the *lie down* and *get up* orders he learned in the initial stages in the shed and yard. I also use *get up* as a command when making him approach the sheep. And a rapid calling of *get up* should quicken his pace when moving them.

Until I am fairly confident the dog is enjoying it and going past the sheep at a sensible distance I keep him in this small area. It may be necessary to start off with the sheep a bit further from the fence to ensure that he will go through with ease and finish up behind them at the correct balancing point.

The young dog can then continue his training back in the field, where I gradually begin to increase the distance between myself and the dog. The older trained dog will now be needed only occasionally, in case the youngster gets a bit rash and disturbs the sheep, which can then scatter. The trained dog would then be used to bring the sheep back into line.

THE YOUNGSTER AT WORK

At this stage the young dog is beginning to follow me and my experienced collies at everyday work round the hill. I usually

The young dog waits at the handler's side while the experienced collie steadies the sheep before the 'pupil' is sent off for them.

keep the youngster at my side, for obedience training, while the main dog is working. But sometimes I use the older dog to bring the sheep closer so that the trainee can get a turn after the sheep have been gathered. Even at this stage, however, the young one is not allowed to go too far with them – and it is essential that the young dog is in proper command before being allowed to work with the sheep.

Working with different sheep is very beneficial. I could, by now, be using the youngster on maybe twenty, thirty, forty or fifty sheep, depending on what size of a group I come across on the hill. Occasionally the pup might get more excited when he sees the sheep. But this gives the trainer the chance to see what further tuition he needs. Putting the dog in a different field with new sheep, is a good way to prepare him for the new experiences of everyday sheep work.

When I finish up a session's tutoring I always end with something which the dog likes to do and can do in an organised fashion. This makes the youngster inclined to look forward to his next training session. It can be a fault of some inexperienced trainers to let the pups do what they want, but it can also be a bad thing to have too much discipline because you will just not get going in the correct way.

The handler should always be standing in a position where the trainee dog can see him.

GIVING COMMANDS

One essential thing is always to give the commands from a position where the dog can see you, so that he does not need to stretch to look over the top of the sheep.

There are collies, especially at sheep dog trials, which continually look back at their handlers for commands. Perhaps one reason is that the trainer used his hands or a stick to signal to him too much at some earlier point in his training. The only time I use a stick as an indicator is to ward the dog off when he is determined to be too close to the sheep.

I never hit dogs with the stick but I will sometimes wave the crook in front of them to get their attention and also threaten them a little. If a young dog needs reprimanding I would never think of using the stick, rather I would put him on his lead and give him a shaking. Keeping him on the lead and finishing the session for the day will give him some time to think about his mistakes. Should you let him off the lead after reprimanding him the pup might disappear out of reach. He might not go home into his kennel because he knows he has done wrong and he will think he is going to get the same again.

6 Fetching

Before a young pup can fetch sheep any distance at all it is essential that he should be doing the work I have described in previous chapters. He should be going round sheep, have a reasonably good stop, be able to walk up and move the sheep a short distance and steer them right or left according to my *come by* and *kway tae me* commands. And, very importantly at this stage, I want the dog to come cleanly away from the sheep when I call *that'll dae*. Until I get all these phases well achieved I do not proceed any further.

THE LIFT

The young dog will then be ready to learn the first stage of the fetching process. This stage, known as the lift, teaches the dog where to end his outrun and begin to bring the sheep forwards.

My method is to run the young collie out first on one side and then the other to get him accustomed to going on both sides. Dogs – especially young ones – can be very much like humans, and they will have a preference for either the right or left side. It can take a little time to get them to understand that they have to be able to go out for sheep on both sides.

I begin teaching the lift by lengthening the distance between the sheep and myself. The dog will be more or less at my feet, or 'at hand' as we term it. He has to leave my feet for his outrun and finish up at 12 o'clock, or the point of balance, at the far side of the stock. Often, I will let a young dog on his outrun go further round the sheep than the correct point of balance, to prevent him stopping too early. If I do want him to stop, for example, before he comes to 12 o'clock, this should be easy enough using the stop command which he learned during his earlier tuition.

When teaching the lift, the sheep should be about fifty yards or so away. I set the dog up, preferably standing on his feet. But if he is keen to get away before I tell him I will put him down on the ground as this will steady him and let him concentrate on seeing the ewes or hoggs. Once he is concentrating it is easier to get him to go off on his outrun in the right direction, so at this juncture I do not mind if he starts off from a lying position.

If he is standing I like to have him with his tail-end towards me while he is looking at the sheep. I try and keep nearby fields clear of stock so that all the dog's attention is on the sheep I want gathered. I might give the youngster a slight hiss to indicate to him that the sheep are there and to make sure that he gets to know this sound.

I step forwards very slowly so that I do not disturb him and then give him a flank command followed by a *s-s-h-s-h* just to encourage him to go right round the sheep fairly smartly. If the pup is going to the right I stand him on my right, and vice versa.

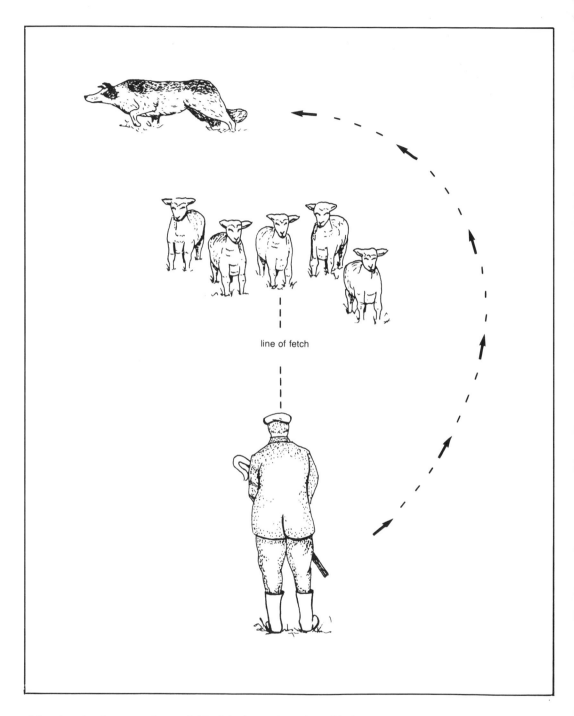

line of fetch

Allowing the dog to go beyond 12 o'clock, or the point of balance,
prevents him from stopping too early.

Dog Too Close

Young dogs starting to gather a flock usually develop all kinds of faults. The most common is that the pup is just too eager to get on with the job. He will then cut corners and come in too close to the sheep at the end of his outrun. To cure this I place the dog further behind me, perhaps about ten yards or so, before I set him off. I order him as previously and always make sure he has seen the sheep.

When I set him off I will start walking to the side of the sheep the dog is heading for and order him further out. I keep doing this until he understands he has to gather the sheep and start the fetch.

When I am satisfied that the dog is going round them at a nice distance I retreat back to where I was originally and I allow him to bring the sheep to me, giving the necessary commands to balance them either on the right or left and bring them fairly directly towards me.

I repeat this exercise until the dog is going out about two hundred yards for the sheep and bringing them back fairly straight. If the dog shows any signs of starting to cut in too closely to the sheep for the lift I immediately shorten the distance he has to fetch them until I get control of the situation again.

The trainer faces the dog to indicate that he is to get further out from the sheep on the flank command.

Fetching

To cure the collie which is inclined to come too close I walk to the side
he is heading for and order him further out.

Dog Too Wide

There have been a few occasions when I have had a young dog which wanted to run out far too wide to fetch sheep. With this type I place the sheep about the distance from the fence or dyke I want the dog to run. I set him up looking at the sheep, but not necessarily with his tail-end turned towards me because he is going wide enough anyway.

When the dog is on the outrun I have a command to keep him from going too wide. I just ask him to *come on up* even while he is running. At this stage all faults have to be dealt with. If the youngster gets away with them the problems will be harder to sort out later on.

Very often the collie which is too wide on his outrun is the one which approaches his sheep too slowly. With this slower type — before the faults are rectified — I would not even stop him at 12 o'clock when gathering and would encourage him to keep coming.

Correct Distance

If for some reason the idea of placing sheep an ideal distance from a fence to tutor the dog to keep the proper distance fails to work, the teaching can be done in the buchts. Another way of educating him about the correct distance from the stock at gathering is to put the sheep into a square corner of a field at a reasonable distance from the fence — say forty or fifty yards. Leave just enough room for the dog to run to the left or right behind the sheep and call him off when he has gathered them and moved them a short distance. As with all the exercises, this should be repeated a few times.

It is preferable to keep some distance between the dog and the sheep when he lifts them, as this will encourage him to gather any straggling stock when at work on the farm, once he is trained.

FLANKING FOR THE FETCH

When starting to bring the sheep on the fetch towards me I ask the dog to flank. If he does not respond and continues to follow the sheep straight on, I stop him on the spot and go right up to him, getting between sheep and dog. I face the dog and ask him to flank, ordering him out to where he should have moved the first time I asked. I then stop him there and go back to where I was standing previously. When walking back — the quiet sheep should have remained quite close — I ask the dog on again, and go through the same procedure. If he flanks when I tell him, I am happy enough, but if not I go back to him again. If the dog is flanking too tightly, a similar method will make sure that he allows the extra distance and does not disturb the sheep.

It is very worthwhile spending a bit of time getting him to flank when told. At this stage I do not bother too much about the accuracy of the flanks. My main aim is simply to get him to flank when the sheep are moving or when they stop and also to learn to flank round behind them.

Most dogs will automatically want to go to the head of the sheep as they have been taught to do this right from the start, in order to stop the sheep from moving away. The dog must now learn to go behind just as freely as he would go to the head of the flock.

PACE

I do not bother too much about the pace at this point as long as the dog is not bringing the sheep too swiftly. I like to see them coming at a nice trot. If the dog is moving too fast I stop him and try and steady him a little. He should not be steadied too much, however, until he is a bit more mature – I have found through my own mistakes that the dog can be reluctant to go on if he is slowed down too much too quickly at an early age.

There are young collies which might not want to go quickly enough. To rectify this I would change the quiet sheep for some that have not become used to dogs. Such sheep will move with less pressure, hence the dog does not need to be so close. This usually works quite well and in no time they will be hurrying to catch up with the sheep. Another way is to try the youngster on four or five sheep rather than the ten or so they have been used to – again, the smaller number will probably move more freely.

ENTHUSIASM

If I have any difficulty getting a young dog to start going to gather sheep at a short distance I bring the sheep closer with my trained dog, turn them around and drive them away with the young dog looking on. This usually encourages the youngster to go and I just let him go when I see him wanting to run.

He may go more or less any way at all, whether it be too close to the sheep or too far off – the main thing is to get him to gather the sheep. I will not start to straighten out any faults until I get him gathering and fetching willingly and

enjoying the job. If a collie at this stage is not quite so sharp and keen as he should be, I leave him longer fetching the sheep more or less in his own way.

If you start to rectify any faults in a dog before he is keen it can make him less interested, and you will find his training going back rather than progressing. I have seen this error made over and over again.

It is possible that the dog may be over-enthusiastic, so it is important to make certain that the dog gives the sheep a wide berth when you call him off with the *that'll dae* command and have him return to you after fetching. My current international Roy is so keen to do what I tell him that if I were to call him off when he is round the back of the sheep, he would come straight through them. I have to flank him off the sheep when I want him to come back to me.

If I am in a large field, when I call the young dog off I give him some praise, walk a short distance down the field and send him away again. Otherwise I drive the sheep back with the trained dog to where they were.

WHISTLE COMMANDS

It is at this stage of training that I introduce the young dog to whistle commands, giving the voice commands he has learned followed by the new whistle orders. The main reason for putting the dog on to whistles is because I do not have a good carrying voice.

When stopping the dog I give the *lie down* command followed by a long continuous whistle. For the approach to the sheep and when fetching them, my whistle notes for *walk on* are two short sharp whistles. The *come by* call is just one

When the dog is called off the sheep on the fetch he must keep wide away from them as he returns to his master.

note repeated, while for *kway tae me* I have a longer note which is repeated. When giving the vocal command followed by the whistles I always call the dog's name too.

Usually collies are quite quick to pick up the whistle commands. In 1957 when I won my first ever Scottish National Trials championship at Dunoon with Roy he was only answering to vocal commands. I put him on to whistle

orders between then and the International Trials which were only three weeks later. He finished fourth in the qualifying round and was runner-up in the supreme championship.

When watching Welshman Ivor Hadfield running in the doubles championship at the 1957 International, I thought it was the finest example of sheep dog handling one could ever wish to see, with his two dogs, Jean and Roy, working perfectly to the different whistles.

I decided there and then I was going to emulate his expertise. As I already had Roy on whistles I started to put his full brother Hope on a different set of notes.

The following year I won the doubles event with the pair at the Scottish National Trials at Kelso and later was second in the International at Dundee – to none other than Ivor Hadfield.

7 Driving

The dog must be taught to drive sheep — especially at a distance for normal hill or field work. Training the youngster to drive should be fairly easy if the learner is obeying all the commands taught previously.

I start by having the trainee dog beside me. I ask him to walk on as I walk with him behind the group of sheep, then I gradually move away from him. For the next two or three sessions I just try and get him to walk on and follow the sheep around wherever they go without any flanking movements at all. I only stop him if he wants to overtake the sheep and go to the head of the flock, as most young dogs are inclined to do. He has, after all, been encouraged to go to the head and fetch sheep to me up to now. He must now learn to stay behind them and take the sheep away from the trainer.

Training the dog to drive can be done at any time in his tuition. I do it whenever I see the opportunity, with the sheep going past me and the dog in position to let him follow on. I only allow him to do this for a few yards each time —

The handler level with the dog, close to the fence to keep him from passing the sheep during tuition in driving.

The handler is now falling back, allowing the dog to control the sheep when learning to drive.

if it works, he is actually driving them before he has noticed, using only the commands of *get up*, *stop* and *lie down*.

I allow the sheep to drift on and then ask the dog to *get up* again. This time I will flank him round to the head of the sheep and have him bring them back. Then I let them go past me to the opposite side. This allows the dog to walk behind the sheep, and I can then move to the other side to walk with him. Again I go through the same procedure of having him get up and then lie down.

I always walk level with the dog so that he knows where I am, and this prevents him getting into a bad habit of looking back over his shoulder. Gradually I work my way back behind him

when he has the confidence to go on himself with the sheep as I repeat the *get up* commands. At this juncture I still allow him to take the sheep anywhere they want to go. Occasionally I will use a trained dog to push the sheep. This stops a youngster getting soured by asking him to put too much power or pressure on the sheep to shift them.

FLANKING ON THE DRIVE

Once the dog has mastered the drive, I start to bring in flanking commands – the same commands he knows for fetching the sheep or circling round them

On the early stages of the drive I walk level with the dog so that he knows where I am. This also prevents him from looking back.

I gradually work my way behind the dog when he has confidence to go on with the sheep.

When walking away, if the dog is on my right I give him the *kway tae me* order.

clockwise or anticlockwise. He must now learn how to respond to these on the drive.

As the dog walks away on the drive with the sheep, if he is on my right and slightly in front of me, I give him the *kway tae me* call. As he takes the command he will go further out from me, but when he has gone a few yards I order him to go down. I let him lie a few seconds then tell him to *get up*. While he is walking with the sheep, I keep a nice distance behind him, and gradually move from his left, behind him to his right, speaking or whistling the commands to *walk on*. He should not have noticed me going to his other side.

I then move up on his right side, level with him, and call *come by*. He should again take this fairly easily as he is moving away from me once more. I will then stop him when he has moved out a few yards. I do not let the youngster get too far out on the wing as this makes it difficult to get him to walk on again.

These manoeuvres are repeated. Going behind the pup all the time makes it easier to have him flank freely in front of me and behind the sheep when taking them away. I only practise for about ten minutes or so at each session and always finish up by allowing the pup to go to the head of the sheep and fetch them back. This prevents the dog looking back on

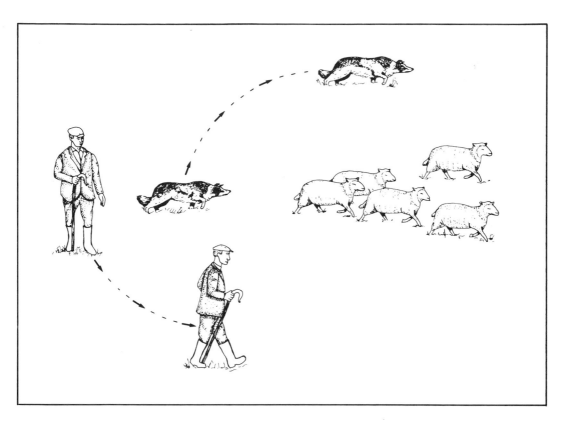

I move from the dog's left behind him to the right before giving him the
order *come by* to the alternative side.

the drive awaiting the *that'll dae* command.

Another method I have tried when
starting a dog to drive is to put sheep
alongside a fence with the collie between
me and the fence. I encourage him to
walk up behind the sheep with myself
level alongside him. I then give him a
flanking command towards the fence,
which stops him going too far round. It
is then much easier to stop him and get
him to walk on again.

While he is walking on I move behind
him, between him and the fence, and
flank him out into the open field to the
head of the sheep. I follow him, and
when he gets to the head of the sheep I

stop him and have him walk on again,
only this time he will be following the
sheep. On this flank round to the head of
the group I try and stop him before he
gets near the fence to allow for another
practice flank towards the fence before
stopping him.

The size of the field where you are
teaching the youngster to drive does not
really matter if you have sheep which
settle and work reasonably well. But the
chance for an extra practice will often
crop up when a shepherd or farmer is
going round doing ordinary hill work —
when the sheep have been gathered, turning them round will often involve driving
them away. At this stage I would not

Driving

The dog has to return from one lot of sheep to bring in another bunch –
sometimes they can be hidden in a hollow or behind a knowe.

have the dog try to drive them through any man-made obstacles. This will come later when trials work is being considered.

Driving is against a dog's natural instincts to begin with, but there should really not be any big problems in getting the youngster to adapt to it. When you are able to incorporate a bit of driving into everyday work with young dogs, the teaching process is less monotonous, as you are likely to be on different ground with different sheep and away from the coaching area. There is certainly much more variety out on the hill.

I use voice and whistle all the time in the driving tuition. I always work fairly close to the sheep because they should be quiet to allow the dog to be quite near them.

Always try and let the young dog do as much as possible on his own without commands. The object is not to over-command, and he should be allowed to use his initiative, but by all means command him if he is going to go wrong. Allowing the youngster to use his own initiative will be an important factor later on in a hill dog, as he can be out of your sight while gathering or driving. Many hill shepherds still drive their stock up the hill at night and the collie has a premier role here. Such a dog will be driving each day and must be as good as possible at his job.

I have never had much trouble teaching dogs to drive but on one occasion I remember only too well that I had quite a challenge with the Moodie's Nap son Nap. I could get him behind the sheep and he would take them away from me in a rather bold manner. He would stop

The art of driving is exemplified here as John competes in a run-off decider to win the driving championships at the 1983 Scottish National Trials. Roy is deftly putting the sheep through the driveaway gate.

fairly well when I told him, but when I asked him to flank the only thing he had in his mind was to get to the front of the sheep.

He would squeeze past between the sheep and the fence or even go through the fence. He completely ignored my stop when asked to flank and on one occasion when the sheep were tightly up against the fence he went over the top of them as he would have done in the buchts. This, in fact, was a great asset when required to turn the sheep back in the pens.

In this case, however, I had no alternative but to put him on a long lead and just go through the same routine along the fence. The cord did the trick – I would check him with it and after he stopped I walked up to him and gave him some praise to let him know he was doing what was required.

I worked with the cord on him for quite a long time. Eventually I took Nap into the centre of a field and kept the cord in my hand with a little tension on it, while he was walking on with the sheep. When I wanted him to flank to me I put a little more weight on the cord and pulled him gently towards me, giving the correct flanking order at the same time. And when I flanked him away from me I had the cord in my hand to stop him. After some time I let the cord trail on the ground and it gave him the impression I still held it in my hand. He began to learn better and progressed more rapidly.

I do not particularly like to use the cord when I get them to this stage because I expect to have them in command. Occasionally, however, a trainer will come across a dog with the eagerness and determination of Nap.

DRIVING CATTLE

Over and over again I have heard people say they never need to have a dog which can drive stock. But on most hills the occasion will arise almost daily when a dog is required to drive sheep to a particular point, whether it be through a ford, over a burn or bridge, or even round the side of a wet boggy area. It is essential that collies are taught to drive.

Dairy farmers might not feel it necessary for a dog to be able to drive as they might only need him to gather the milking cows twice daily. Even so, at one time, when our family milked cows in the old-fashioned byre with cows chained in their stalls, I released eight cows at a time after they were milked. The dog would drive the cows one hundred yards back to their field.

One of my dogs, Buff, son of my 1972 International supreme champion Cap, was very good at taking considerable numbers of cattle back to the fields. I would not even need to look out to see where he was. As soon as the cows were released he would fold in behind them and drive them nicely to the field. If the cattle stopped he would heel one of them and if they went past the gate he would go beyond and head them. Usually he would nip a nose to turn them and heel again several times. Then he would return to the farmstead to wait for the next lot.

My Moss dog works a lot with dairy cattle. He goes down the cubicles and brings them all up at once into the collecting area. He will sit in the cubicles and often comes to see if more are ready to be taken back to the fields. Dogs can get very keen on this kind of routine.

8 Shedding

Just as it is essential to have a working collie which will drive stock, the shepherd or farmer will require a dog which can shed or cut out a sheep from a flock. In fact, he will hardly encounter a day when this skill is not needed.

There are many reasons why a particular sheep may have to be separated from the rest on a hill farm. It may be that at tupping time the ram has strayed from his own heft (a geographical area on a hill farm) on to another. It is then necessary to get him away from the ewes there and drive him back to his own territory to attend to the work allotted to him. At other times a ewe may be needing attention – she could be ailing or needing help to lamb. Here again a dog which can shed out a particular sheep is required.

The time when a really good shedding dog is a necessity is during the lambing season, with ewes which are having problems. It could also be that a newly-born lamb is not suckling, a dog would then be needed to shed off the mother so that the lamb could be put to her teats. In

'This one'. John Templeton is down to cutting out the last uncollared sheep in his run at the Lockerbie International with Roy in 1985.

short – where there are sheep a shedding dog is essential.

When I train a dog to shed I like to use a fair number of sheep in the initial stages, possibly twenty or thirty. The reason for this is that a group this size is less likely to try to get back together when they are split into two lots as the dog comes in between them. A smaller bunch of sheep – say eight – would be more inclined, once separated, to move back together again.

I start this stage of tuition by gathering the sheep with the young dog and fetching them as closely as possible to me without disturbing them too much. I make the dog lie with the *lie down* command at his side of the sheep and then I work my way through the middle of the flock towards him. My aim is to have half the sheep going either way, and I try

to make the opening fairly wide until the two groups are going away in opposite directions.

I then call the dog, saying *that'll dae* followed by the command *come in*, which is my order for shedding. When the dog comes in almost to me I put him down and retreat myself. I allow him to take control of one lot of sheep, preferably the group that is moving away most easily. The dog is allowed to drive them away a short distance – I will help him do this myself if necessary and make sure none of the sheep burst back and try to reach the other group.

This task should always be made as easy as possible in the initial shedding lessons. I repeat the job a few times, gathering the sheep once again with the dog and splitting them myself. But when I ask the dog to come through, I

Starting to train the collie to shed sheep by asking him to come through the main group with the *that'll dae* command.

The collie now takes two sheep off and makes sure they are going away easily from the main bunch.

gradually phase out the command *that'll dae* and use only *come in*. Using *that'll dae* to begin with allows the dog to come freely to me. This command, I must stress, should never be used for anything other than getting the dog to return, as serious trouble can be caused through confusing him.

If by chance the sheep want to break back to join their mates when I bring the young dog in, I will call up the experienced dog that I always have out on the hill with me. I would use him to stop the sheep rather than have the young dog attempt the job, as the youngster would be more than likely to end up seizing hold of a sheep when taken by surprise as they charged past him.

Should I not have an experienced dog with me I would call the young collie off and start all over again. But the object is

to try and avoid this situation as much as possible.

SHEDDING A SINGLE SHEEP

The youngster should gradually be gaining confidence and coming in freely when I ask him. Each time I cut off fewer sheep from the thirty. Gradually I work towards the point where I am asking the trainee dog to come in and take off two at the end of the bunch.

Finally, when I make the first attempt to shed off a single sheep I try and make sure it is the one going away or preparing to go away from the dog without any wearing or forcing. This makes it easier for the youngster. When I want the dog to shed off the single sheep I change the

Shedding

The last sheep is split off.

The important task of 'wearing' a sheep – driving it from the main flock and making sure it does not rejoin the others.

command to *come in, this yin* (come in, this one).

I continue to do this for a few sessions before asking him to come in and cut off a single sheep that is facing him, which will require to be 'worn' – faced up to and prevented from running – or forced to go away from the main flock. Even at this stage I would be close at hand to help if the sheep tried to beat him and re-join the flock. The youngster has not yet had enough experience to stop this single ewe; he may turn tail or even grip her if tested too severely. He will eventually stop the sheep which wants to break back but this will never be achieved without practice to gain confidence.

Occasionally a breaking sheep will appear when a shepherd or farmer is putting a flock through a gate or shepherding them into the buchts. There is always the odd one looking for her freedom. But this one will usually turn back to her mates quite easily when the dog takes charge and shows his authority. Jobs like this help the youngster to gain experience and confidence all the time without trying to rush him into it.

PRACTISING SHEDDING

Some dogs tend to be quicker at picking up the shedding phase. It can be a difficult skill to teach because the accent has up to now been on keeping the dog from coming too close to the sheep, yet he is suddenly being asked to come in among them. A dog which has been inclined to go in among the sheep at an earlier stage will be more difficult to teach because he has been schooled and scolded to keep out.

An ideal time for trying shedding is at everyday work. In fact, as the different phases of training are added, I find that more and more of the tuition comes during the completion of daily chores, except at critical times of the year.

Sometimes when I have gathered and checked sheep I let the young dog drive them away from me before going on to the next lot just to let him gain experience. And again, if the chance arises, I will have him shed off some of the sheep. It also gets the trainee collie away from the routine of being in the same field with the same stock.

USES OF SHEDDING

A good job for the young dog which is getting well on in his training is to work in the buchts forcing the sheep, for instance, through the shedder or the race (parts of the more modern sheephandling facilities aimed at giving freer movement and access to sheep). Here in the pens one sheep may occasionally try and get away from the back of the flock, but she can be easily turned with a command to the dog to stop her.

Even when working in the buchts with a young dog I will have an experienced collie with me. This makes it easier for the younger one to be confident when he is turning a breaking sheep without gripping or turning tail. Shedding is a phase of work which a dog becomes very keen on after he masters the art of turning a breaking sheep. Make sure he is in proper command, though, or he may become so keen that he will just dive in if he sees a space.

The shedding dog can be very useful on a dairy farm. A big number of milk producers overwinter the hoggs belonging to hill farmers. Sometimes these farms are not fenced adequately for sheep and the hoggs tend to slip through and join those on a neighbouring farm. If the farmer does not have a dog which can shed and hold sheep, the hoggs might have to be taken into pens before the straying ones can be returned to their own flocks.

GRIPPING

Gripping is simply allowing the dog to give the sheep a quick nip, usually in the wool. Dogs should only do this on command, otherwise it can become a habit. My order is *take hold*.

Occasions on which I would tell my dog to grip are, for instance, when turning a stubborn sheep which just refuses to respond unless gripped, or to catch a ewe which requires attention at lambing time. Gripping can also be necessary to encourage sheep up the shedder if they have stopped and they need to be moved further. Another occasion when I do not mind a dog gripping is if I am filling up the catching pen at dipping time. Older ewes smell the dip and refuse to go into the small catching pen, having been twice through the dipper each year and not relished the experience.

I do not, however, work with a young dog at lambing time. I may have one with me, but I always use the experienced collie to catch sheep. If the young dog is taught to hold or grip the sheep at this time it can be difficult to break him of the habit, because he will very quickly become used to it. A ewe at lambing time is not usually too difficult to catch, but it is not really a job for a young dog to hold her.

The Roy dog which won the 1957 Scottish National Trials just would not grip, even when ordered. In the pen, when commanded to grip he would run at sheep and hit them with his shoulder.

9 Go Back

The working dog must be able to return from one group of sheep and pick up another batch in some far corner of a field or even out of sight on the hill. This, too, is an essential task the collie may face every day. This skill has been left almost to the end of the basic training schedule, but it is nevertheless important to train the young dog to turn back and gather these other sheep in an organised manner.

I never hurry to train the young dog to return, as he can become too keen on turning back. It is also important that he is fairly well trained in all other aspects of his work before I begin to train him to turn back over a longer distance. A trainer must be very careful that the pup does not start to leave his first flock of sheep for another lot before he gets the proper command to do so. Also, the trainer should always work the young dog at a distance where he is under control. When the dog gets too far away he is more inclined to take advantage and perhaps do things wrongly.

The need to have a dog that will turn back for more stock arises quite frequently on the hill farm when gathering. Often the dog will have missed some sheep which are out of his sight, perhaps in a hollow or behind a knowe or even among heather or rushes. These sheep have to be gathered as well.

On the dairy farm quite often cows run in more than one field. When the dog is gathering the first field, he may be asked to go back and be guided through a gate into the next field to bring the remainder of the cows. Sometimes during the summer the dairy herd at Airtnoch has access to three neighbouring fields. The gates are all left open and it saves a lot of walking if I can send the dog out through the three fields just by directing him to the appropriate spots.

TEACHING THE RETURN

The first step I take when teaching the dog to return is to gather the sheep and fetch them up in front of me. I shed these into two droves. I then walk away and make the dog bring one lot of sheep behind me for a short distance — far enough away from the other lot to prevent them from wanting to rejoin the group, but not too far so that I can get the young dog to see the bunch he has left behind without too much trouble. With the sheep stopped and the dog lying down I go round to where the dog is sitting and manoeuvre him to look for the first lot which we left behind.

In the early stages of this training when I am moving him round to set his sights on the second lot of sheep I put him to the ground if he shows edginess, even when he is looking for the sheep. It is nicer if he stands, but if you cannot hold him make him sit until he gets his eyes on the sheep.

I say *that'll dae* to get him on his feet and then use the command I have to alert

Go Back

The dog has to return from one lot of sheep to bring in another bunch
– sometimes they can be hidden in a hollow or behind a knowe.

the dogs to the fact I will be sending them back for more sheep: *come 'ere*. This may seem a strange command to indicate that the dog is going to go further away from me, but I have always used it successfully.

When this command has alerted his attention to the sheep that have to be gathered, I give him the flank command, either *kway tae me* or *come by* on the side I want him to go. At this stage it is usually the direction he is angling to go, as this will enable me to get him started without too much fuss.

I allow him to gather this group of sheep and, while he is fetching them, I move back round to the other side of the group of sheep which he had brought to me originally. This means that the dog, both lots of sheep and myself are now in a straight line. I let the dog bring the sheep he is with and join the two groups together. Then I call him away with the *that'll dae* command. I do not usually repeat this lesson again the same day but wait until the next time I get the opportunity and go through the same procedure again.

After a few practice runs I gradually give him the command to turn back without going too near him, though just close enough to make sure I am in control of the situation. He must turn around when I say *come 'ere* and stop on the ground or on his feet and not fly away back for the other sheep. When he is turned round and I see him eyeing the sheep to be gathered I give him the command and ensure he does not leave until he gets that order.

I use the whistle command for the actual go-back – basically a whistled version of *come 'ere* with two distinctive notes – after I get him going back fairly well to the voice commands. The whistle is better for turning him back on long

The dog glances back as he is taught to turn and gather more sheep.

distances and on bigger areas. I gradually lengthen the distance the dog has to go back by splitting the sheep with my trained dog and placing them well apart in the field or on the hill. Usually, I gather the nearest group with the young dog. At this stage I still bring the sheep close to me to ensure I get him turned properly and have full control to guide him left or right.

When I start to repeat the turn back – that is if I am still in the same field – I place the two groups of sheep in a different position each time to prevent the trainee dog from getting into a routine.

It is not really difficult to teach the collie to go back. If all the other orders are being obeyed it is fairly simple, and I always find it an interesting phase of the training work. If, by chance, the young dog does not turn back when asked, you should not scold him or check him too severely. If you continually reprimand him for failing to turn back, he may come to associate the two and begin to go back every time you check him, whether you ask him to or not.

RETURNING FOR HIDDEN SHEEP

If there happens to be a hollow or somewhere I can put one group of sheep out of sight, I gather the first visible group and then direct the dog to where the second group are hidden, guiding him with commands as he goes.

Having gathered the second bunch of stock he now brings them to join his first group.

At this stage I am not too bothered about which side he goes to lift that second bunch. My main aim is to get him to turn back and go for the sheep, perhaps without seeing them. If he knows he is going to find sheep which he cannot see when I turn him back, I start to train him to go either right or left on the way back to make sure he lifts the sheep on the side I require.

I do this by turning him off the first lot and then stopping him. I go to where the dog is and if I am going to start him to the right I stand on his left side and command him *kway tae me*, let him go a short distance – say fifty yards or so – and stop him again. I then move behind him on his right side and flank him to the left saying *come by*. He will still be looking towards where the sheep are hidden as he knows by this time he will find them there. This time I let him go right on round and collect them. I repeat this and the next time I turn him back I let him lift the sheep on the right side.

To let him gain more experience, I take the chance when going round the hill perhaps to look for two groups of sheep. Instead of letting him go right round the two groups I call him in beyond the first bunch and make him fetch them to me. Then I practise turning him back for the second group.

The open hill is the best place to practise sending the dog back because very seldom will you come across two groups of sheep in the same position. If, when I turn a dog back, he does not return to the side I ask him, I halt the dog and walk towards him. It is then easier to make him do as I ask.

The best dog I ever had at going back for a second group of sheep was Fleet. However, because he never got in the Scottish team for the singles at the International Trials he never had the chance to show his skill at the double lift test, held on the final day of the supreme championship.

10 That Extra Polish

Having gone through all the phases of training a young dog, I will have made up my mind if he is good enough to go with me to sheep dog trials or if he is going to be a good everyday work dog.

If I decide he will be a work dog I will keep him until he has a little more practical experience and sell him when I find a buyer. There will always be a market for the good sheep and cattle dog.

What I am looking for in the trials dog is a bit of class and style; a dog which is quick to act and slow to lose his temper. He has to be a good listener and have that little extra bit of ability. The dog's abilities will be inherited and not man-made, and the trainer must be capable of taking advantage of these natural abilities to be successful. He must be determined to succeed, and have a deep love for the border collie. He must have control and authority at all times.

John Templeton's collies ready for a day trip to a sheep dog trial.

If a dog is too plain, carrying its head too high and with not enough power of eye to steady it, this can relegate it from being considered for trials. I like an attractive dog for work on the trials tasks – I like to see nice action and carriage. There are sometimes points about good working dogs – flagging their tails at turns for instance – which will be penalised on the trials field, but are acceptable on hill, field or pen work.

It gives me a tremendous feeling of satisfaction to handle a well-trained trials dog. But this is not to detract from the good commercial work dog, which is one of the most important tools of the livestock industry.

TRAINING FOR TRIALS

Assuming the dog is taking all the various commands and working pleasantly, showing promise of making a trials dog, extra polish must be given to his skills before he is ready for competition.

I go right back to the beginning and gradually work to instil a little more discipline. I like the dog to be about one-and-a-half years old before I begin training for trials. Unlike some trainers, I never have a trials course set up at home, as tutoring them on laid-out courses becomes too much of a routine which will get mechanical actions into the youngsters.

Instead, I use an imaginary course when I am walking about the farm. I choose particular landmarks or geographical features. With the dog following closely at my side I more or less pretend I am at a trial, walking out to the handler's post. I then give the dog a hiss, my command to let him know there are sheep further out on the field or hill and that he has to look for them.

I usually use five or six hoggs for the advanced training. On the outrun I like the dog to give the sheep a little more room as he goes round to lift them at the far end. It may simply be a case of giving him a few extra commands to keep him further out and then gradually dropping these orders as he gets to know he has to be slightly further off the stock. Then if he knows the line to take on the outrun he will not need commands. It is important, however, not to overdo the orders.

I let him go on the outrun a few times to either side, just to find out what alterations, if any, are needed. If he is coming in too tight to the sheep at the far end, I will keep at him and widen him out gradually, even when going round a hill. It is just a matter of ordering him back as he goes round the sheep.

He must stop when asked and not run on a few yards after he gets the stop whistle. If he does not stop when ordered and goes on past the balancing point on the outrun at a trial he will be penalised with a points deduction. Stopping at the correct balancing point is important here as the dog must bring the sheep straight towards the obstacles or gates which have to be negotiated on the fetch part of the trials course.

When lifting the sheep to start them off on the fetch the dog must come boldly when asked, showing his power to move his charges. He must not come too fast, as this can disturb the sheep and send them away down the field.

If the sheep go off line on the fetch, the dog will be commanded to straighten them up. Again, he must turn off them that little bit wider than he has been used to on his training flanks. This is to get the sheep moving as quietly as possible. When out on the flank he must stay there

That Extra Polish

Often when out at everyday work John goes to an imaginary trials post.

Keeping a steady pace as the sheep are brought through fetch obstacles.

Driving away to negotiate one of the obstacles.

if asked to stop and not swing back behind the sheep again as this would put the animals further off the course

I ask the dog to come straight on, to line the sheep up towards the fetch gates. Fewer points will be taken off if the sheep remain quiet and are moved in a straight line. The same applies when driving away, the phase which begins after the sheep – having been brought down through the fetch gates – have been put round behind the handler. If a flank is needed, I ask the dog to flank at right angles to the sheep to try and get them going quietly towards the next obstacle, which is the first gate on the drive.

After the sheep are through the gate, they have to be turned as closely as possible to head them for the second drive flakes. A change of the whistled tone will put that extra urgency into a command if needed at this point. The orders to get the sheep lined up for the cross drive can be a flank to either right or left depending on the way the trials course has been set up. So when practising on my imaginary course I have the dog flank first to the left side and then to the right.

When turning at the drive gates the dog will have to come cleanly off the sheep and flank round to line them up for the second drive gates. He will then take them quietly through and again turn neatly to head the sheep straight back towards the pen. If the lines between the obstacles are kept straight, and the turns after going through gates kept tight, fewer points will be lost. The sheep should always be kept at a nice steady pace or even a trot.

Wearing sheep up towards the pen.

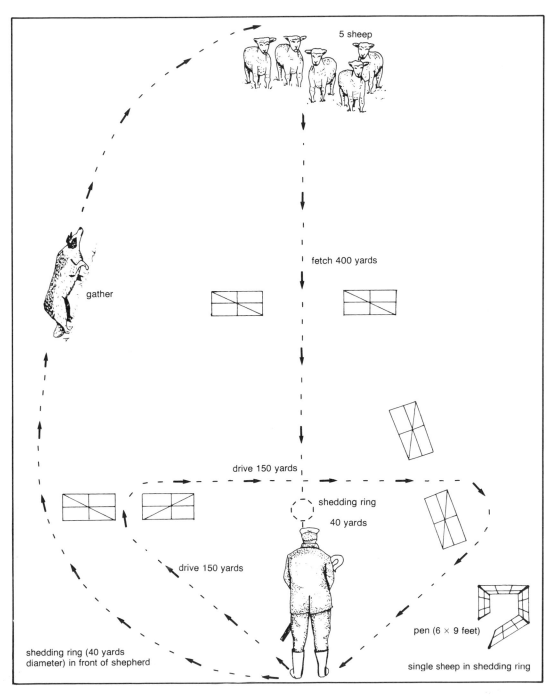

The course at the National Sheep Dog Trials. The same course is used in the qualifying round of the International Trials. Diagram courtesy of the International Sheep Dog Society.

NATIONAL TRIALS

In a National or International Trial the sheep will be brought straight to the shedding ring after passing through the final drive gates. They must be brought into this ring – which is usually marked out by heaps of sawdust – before the handler leaves his commanding post. Two of the five sheep will be wearing coloured collars buckled round their necks and the first stage here is to shed two of the unmarked ones from the group. The handler has to manoeuvre the sheep about quietly, taking care they do not get out of the ring. He must then make an opening for the dog to come through and cut off the two sheep, which the dog then controls.

At the national event the dog would then send the sheep back to the group. The handler moves to the pen to open the gate which he will have tied with rope. The dog brings the five sheep to the mouth of the pen and the handler, who is allowed to hold the rope, and the collie co-operate to work the sheep into the pen. All the dog's previous experience will come into force here to prevent them bursting away. The dog will use his power to push these sheep into the pen.

To complete the national course the sheep are released from the box and the dog drives them back into the shedding ring where the task is to shed one which is wearing a collar. The sheep have to be settled down and the collared one manoeuvred to one end. The handler will try

Concentration by man and dog at the pen as John and his old Roy dog get ready to pen at Neilston sheep dog trials in 1975. John won that day with Roy – and also won the Ayrshire cattle championship. The trial is unusual in that the handler holds the gate rope with his right arm.

The dog finally pushes the sheep into the pen.

John Templeton always takes the dog with him round to the back of the pen before releasing the sheep.

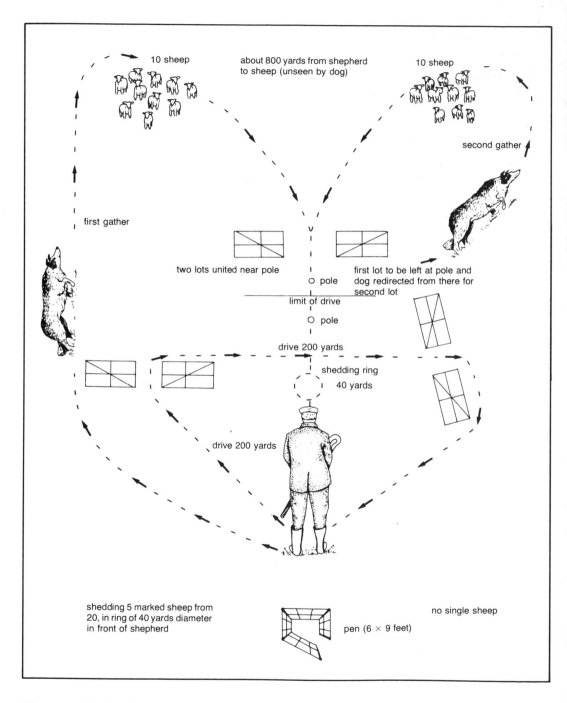

The course for the final day at the International Sheep Dog Trials
– the supreme championship for which fifteen handlers qualify.
Diagram courtesy of the International Sheep Dog Society.

to make a space for the dog to come in, cut out the single sheep and then wear it (hold it steady) to the satisfaction of the judges.

At the normal open sheep dog trials there may be only three or four sheep to work with, and they do not have collars. If the rules of the organising society stipulate that a single sheep has to be shed off then it should be the last one going past the handler.

When I shut the gate of the pen at trials I call the dog to my feet and keep him there, even when walking round the back of the pen to chase the sheep back out. I never let the dog go to the back of the pen himself. If collies are at trials every weekend they could get into the habit of doing this, and could be likely to make the mistake of going to the back of the pen before the sheep are completely inside. This would turn them out again, and cause a big deduction of points.

INTERNATIONAL TRIALS

The supreme championship course on the final day of the International Trials is much bigger than the national layout. To begin with, ten sheep are placed about eight hundred yards from the handler. They have to be lifted by the collie and brought into the centre of the course through the fetch gates. The dog is then commanded to leave them there and is redirected back for a second bunch of ten sheep in the opposite corner of the course. These will also have to be brought through the fetch gates, and then joined up with the first flock.

The score of sheep are then driven as one flock round the drive and back into the shedding ring where fifteen without

collars have to be run off and the dog and handler left with five sheep wearing collars or ribbons. The handler then pens these. It has all to be done within thirty minutes.

I remember when I started attending the International Trials only two or three of the handlers reaching the final stage actually completed the full supreme championship course. In more recent years only two or three have failed to finish. That, I feel, settles the argument that dogs must be better now than they were thirty years ago.

BRACE CLASS

Running in the doubles or brace class is just a polished up version of using two dogs together at home for the daily duties. In the brace class at trials one dog is directed to the left and the other to the right on the outrun. Ideally both should arrive at the far end behind the sheep together. One can be stopped at 11 o'clock and one at 1 o'clock, or they can cross over behind the sheep. After that they must stay on the side at which they lifted the sheep all the way down the fetch, round the drive and back to the shedding ring.

Here one dog is stopped and the other brought in close to shed the sheep into two equal droves. One dog will be used to pen the first group and then guard the pen entrance, as there are no gates on these boxes in the brace competition. Then the other dog will bring the second group to the other pen.

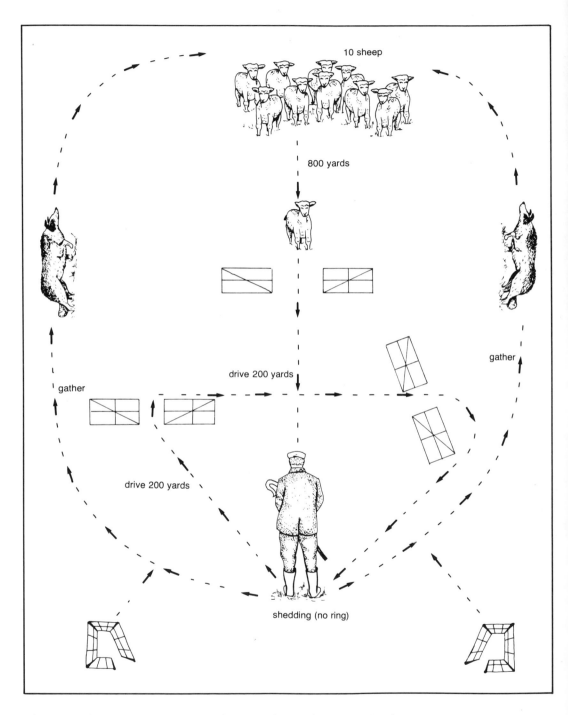

The course for the brace or doubles championship at the International
Trials. Diagram courtesy of the International Sheep Dog Society.

READING SHEEP

A trials dog does not just appear out of the blue. It takes a lot of practice to make perfection in every partnership. But the handler must be capable of reading, or studying the behaviour, of sheep. He must watch them and try and work out what they are about to do long before they do it, and be ready to prevent mistakes which could mean the loss of points.

The best handler of my time at reading sheep was the late Jimmy Millar. I am sure all handlers who knew him as well as I did will agree that many times, when watching him running dogs at trials, we would wonder why he had made a particular move. Nine times out of ten he would be correct, as we would see later on in the trial – he would just have noticed that the sheep were about to make a move, and had put his dog in position to anticipate this movement.

Reading sheep can be difficult if you are not a stocksperson. When I am tutoring at Agricultural Training Board courses, one of the first things I do is to spend a little time with the pupils trying to get them to understand sheep, respect them and follow the moves they are going to make.

At sheep dog trials handlers come across many different breeds and crosses

Whatever happens on the trials field, it is the everyday practical work that is most important. Here a dog helps to push sheep into the shedding race at Airtnoch.

of sheep which will all need a different approach from the dog and, therefore, a different attitude and commands from the handler. A trials entrant never knows until he starts his trial what the sheep will be like. Sheep will also react differently to the various types of dogs and their style, movement and power. A bold, strong dog, for instance, is inclined to disturb the sheep just that little bit more than a more kindly dog.

OWNERSHIP CHANGES

At various stages in their lifetime dogs can change ownership. Although most handlers use the same vocal commands, nearly all the whistles differ to a lesser or greater degree. If I acquire a trained dog and the whistles he is accustomed to do not suit me, I work the collie on vocal commands for a time before gradually adding the new whistle orders I have selected for him after the voice commands. This has always worked fairly well.

If a new owner wants to work a dog on the whistles the animal has been used to, the best way is to get a tape recording made by the previous owner with the dog's vocal commands followed by the whistles. In this way the owner can refresh his memory periodically.

11 Judging

Watching practical work with sheep which have been well shepherded and have been put out to the post neatly is the ideal when judging sheep dog trials. Judging can be a pleasure, but it can also be a pain.

When I am judging I deduct a point or points in every phase of work round the trials course if the dog could have done a better job. In other words, every deviation from perfection will lose a point or points depending on the severity of the mistake. My judging hints in this chapter will be on the lines of a National Trial, where there are 20 points for the outrun, 10 for the lift, 20 for the fetch, 30 on the drive, 10 for the pen and 10 for the shed.

I always have a clerk to whom I dictate my points deductions. Some judges may write down their own pointings but I prefer to dictate my decisions, for one needs only to glance away for a fraction of a second and something unexpected could have been missed.

It is sometimes a problem for a local trials society to get the ideal sheep, especially nowadays when motor cycles and Land Rovers could be the method of shepherding. But they should always try and get sheep that have been well shepherded.

Putting out the sheep at the top end can also bring problems sometimes, with too many men and too many dogs. I like to see one man and one dog taking the sheep from the holding pen to the post — and preferably a well-trained dog that will stay well back and will come away from the sheep when asked. It can be difficult if the sheep are a bit unruly and want to run off. It is better if the man can stand at the side where the sheep want to go and so head them and keep his dog there until the competing collie comes round to lift the sheep. If the dog is not in the path of the sheep he can be left there until the sheep have been taken by the trials collie out of his reach. Then he can be called off. If the dog holding the sheep is in front he should be called off whenever the competing collie goes round to take control of the flock.

OUTRUN

So to the actual trial. What I like to see when competing as well as judging is the handler walking smartly towards the handler's post with the dog close beside him. The handler should set the dog up to look for the sheep being released at the other end of the course. The dog should be no further away from the handler than approximately 6 feet for a national-size course or approximately 12 feet for a full international run of 800 yards.

If the dog is set up and sent off at a greater distance than this I deduct points accordingly. I would also deduct points if the dog turned back to the handler. Ideally the dog should go away for the sheep, opening out all the way in a more or less pear-shaped outrun arriving at the back of the flock at a distance of roughly

30 yards without disturbing them.

If the sheep move away from the side the dog is running out on, the collie would have to carry on past 12 o'clock to reach the point of balance. This is the spot where he has to stop the sheep and bring them in a direct line towards the fetch gates the shortest way. If the dog stopped at 12 o'clock in this situation — where the sheep had moved to the side — he would lose points as he would have to be commanded round to the point of balance. If the sheep move towards the side the dog is running out on then he would have to be stopped at the point where he is going to line up sheep towards the fetch gate. Again if he goes past this point of balance he would have to be commanded back, so here again he would lose points. This could be anything from one to six points, depending on how many commands he had to correct him.

A command on the outrun taken while running is not a big fault and in my opinion would only lose one point whether it is to turn him out or bring him in, but if he has to be stopped and re-directed he would lose much more, possibly three or four points. I don't particularly like a dog running the dyke or fence on the outrun (that means right alongside these boundaries) for the simple reason that if there was no fence there, where would he go? The only outrun close to a fence I would leave with full points is one where the field was small enough to make this the only option and keep the dog far enough off his sheep on the outrun.

If the dog disappears out of the field altogether I would be very hard on him. If he crosses over between the handler and the sheep and so lifts his flock from the opposite side to which he was directed I would take 19 of the 20 points off, as he has refused his correction commands and defied the handler. If he crosses over and is corrected back on to the side he was on at the start of the outrun I would take at least half the outrun points away and possibly more depending on how many commands it took to correct him. I prefer a dog to be rather too wide than too tight or too straight up the course on the outrun, so I am rather more lenient with the wide outrun but pretty severe on the tight or straight run.

LIFT

When the dog completes his outrun I prefer him to stop at the right point. However, it is not absolutely necessary that he must stop if the handler is confident enough to let him go on, provided he does it correctly, and I would not take anything off in that instance. I like to see the dog approach the sheep steadily but boldly, to move the sheep straight in the direction required at the lift phase. If the dog takes too long to lift the sheep it is often a sign that he has too much eye and points would be lost. Again if he rushes at the sheep points would be deducted, and in this case he would have disturbed the sheep and unsettled them for the remainder of the trial.

Should the collie go in among the sheep at the lift, and I was sure he had gripped a sheep, I would disqualify him. But if I was not sure whether he had taken hold of a sheep I would take all his 10 lift points away. There are also often problems with sheep moving away from their post before the trials dog has arrived. If they move off line before the dog is asked to lift them, his first move should be to flank round to the point where he has to straighten them up.

The vexed question of re-runs often occurs on the outrun/lift phases of the trial. I would not consider a re-run for the handler in any circumstances unless there is some unforeseen happening, like another dog interfering with the sheep while the run is in progress or one of the sheep being found to be unsound. In such cases the time-clock should be stopped and the handler would have to go through the whole trial again on fresh sheep with the pointing only starting where the incident had occurred.

When judging I accept the lift and fetch from the point where the sheep are picked up if they have wandered away from the post, and certainly will not take any points off because the sheep have moved, provided the handler makes a first class job of bringing them back on to the course. The only time I would consider giving a re-run is if the sheep had strayed too far and it was going to take more time than allocated to finish the run.

FETCH

Wherever they are lifted, the sheep should be moved towards the fetch obstacle without over-flanking. If the dog over-flanks he will turn the sheep too far in the opposite direction, which automatically means he will have to flank again to the other side. This would lose him points depending on how often he puts them away from the straight line of the fetch. The dog should stay at a sufficient distance from the sheep to keep them coming with a nice flowing action. If the sheep are light and coming easily

the dog must not go too close or he will be inclined to rush them too much and will lose points. If the sheep are heavy to move he will need to be a lot closer to them and a lot firmer in his actions to keep them moving at a nice pace.

Points will be lost by the handler if he allows the sheep to keep stopping, as he is not properly in control of the situation. The same applies in all the flanks. If the sheep are light he must be wider on his flanks to prevent disturbing the sheep – the opposite applies if the sheep are stiff to bring on. Here the dog must flank a lot closer to his charges to keep them coming. If he flanks wide on stiff sheep they will be more likely to stop and graze and this would mean a further deduction in points. Quite often the dog will flank on his own accord when not required and this too puts the sheep off line, with resultant deductions in the mark-up.

If the fetch obstacle – and other obstacles to come – are missed I will penalise heavily. I usually take two points per sheep plus a point deduction for deviation from the line. My opinion is that if gates and obstacles are set up then the sheep have to be put through them to gather points.

DRIVE

The course director at trials will explain the course to the competitor before he goes to the post, and when the sheep arrive at the end of the fetch they will be turned round the back of the handler to the right or the left according to the trials society's rules to start the drive. If the sheep pass the wrong side of the handler I treat it as I treat a missed obstacle, with two points per sheep taken off. The distance the sheep should pass behind the handler will vary according to the sheep. If they are quiet they should be within five yards of the handler but if they are light and fast I would not take a point off if they were twice that distance away.

A judge has to be practical and if I think in the circumstances a manoeuvre could have been done better, I certainly would take points off. At this point I like to see the dog following the sheep round the handler at a nice distance, to control the sheep and start them off in a straight line to the first obstacle on the drive, where again I do not like a dog over-flanking. This only puts the sheep too far in the opposite direction. I like to see the dog moving steadily and guiding the sheep without too much stopping. I do not really mind a dog going down on the ground when asked to stop so long as he gets up immediately when asked and does not make a habit of going down too much.

When the first drive gates are negotiated the sheep should be turned as closely as possible to the gates and lined up towards the second drive gates. There again there should be a tight turn back to the pen or the sawdust ring for shedding depending on whether it is a national or open trial. On tight close turns round the gates I always take into consideration what the sheep are doing, and judge it as practically as possible.

SHEDDING

The drive ends at the pen or the sawdust shedding ring. That triangle from the first drive obstacle and the second obstacle must be as straight as possible. Every little movement off the line will mean a loss of points where there are 30 to be gained. At the National Trials sheep are brought into the ring and two unmarked ones shed off. Here I like to see the dog come in to shed them off when the opportunity is there and not see the handler moving in first.

Rules for shedding at local trials where sheep are unmarked can vary and the handler will be instructed on this. If it is a split with two sheep being cut off from four, the dog must go in and take control of the two sheep. He must go in smartly and turn preferably on to the two sheep facing him. If he turns on to the two sheep turning away from him that is the easy way out. I would penalise this, but not too severely. But if the handler had been instructed to take the last two sheep then I would be very hard in this situation. I would also deduct a point if I thought the handler had missed a shedding opportunity.

PEN

The next phase at national level is the pen and in this case the five sheep should be re-grouped. The most workmanlike way to do this job is to gather the lot of sheep furthest away from the pen and join them up with those which have been shed off and which are perhaps nearest to the pen. The handler will proceed towards the pen leaving the dog to bring the sheep to the mouth of the pen and work the sheep as quietly as possible into the 'house' without disturbing them or allowing them to burst past the handler or the pen. The handler must not touch the sheep with his stick or pull the gate on to the sheep to push them in, but push them slowly with the dog – preferably on his feet – and gently close the gate, without banging it. I have taken points off in the past for 'mis-use' of the gate.

When the gate is re-opened I like the dog to stay at the side of the pen, either the same side as the handler or the opposite, while the sheep are released. The dog should not rush round to the back of the pen out of control – if this happens I would penalise it. The dog must not pass between the handler and the sheep when collecting the sheep into position for the last phase – the singling – at national level. This entails shedding off one of two marked sheep, and it can be taken off at either end of the small flock. The dog has to be brought in to wear her away from the other four.

At local trials, where perhaps a single unmarked sheep has to be shed off, it will be the last sheep. My definition of this situation is that the dog must come in to the face of the particular sheep and not on to the tail end of the sheep that is turned away. Points will be deducted if opportunities are missed. If the dog came in to take a sheep that was moving away I would at least halve the shedding award. I like a dog to arrive in smartly at the head of the sheep. I do not, when judging, ask that the sheep be turned because some would not turn under any circumstances. If the dog comes in at the first opportunity to head off the sheep I am satisfied and I would award the full 10 points.

FINAL POINTS

When the full course has been completed the handler should immediately gather his sheep – at local trials anyway, as there is usually a dog for the purpose at the national and international events – and proceed with them towards the exhaust pen as smartly as possible in order not to distract the next dog.

A good outrun and lift usually sets up a really good run. If too many points are lost on the outrun and lift it can be very difficult to make up during the remainder of the run. I do not penalise over-commanding too much. I penalise more the dog that is given commands and does not take them. That is worse than a dog being commanded all the time and taking these commands.

There can be times when it seems dogs are provoked into gripping sheep. We often find that a sheep will stand facing the dog. In such circumstances the dog may have to go in and perhaps nip the nose of the sheep to move it. I would tolerate this and would class it as a provoked grip, but an unprovoked grip brings instant disqualification, as does abuse of sheep. You have to keep in mind the owner of the sheep who has kindly loaned them and does not expect them to be abused.

Sometimes judging can be from 7 a.m. to 7 p.m. at open trials and three days of concentration are needed at national and international events. At open trials it is possible to find two handlers on the same points at the top of the prizelist. In these circumstances I would order a run-off between the two to decide who gets the first place. But if one of the handlers has perhaps left the field then I would give first place to the handler who had highest points on the outrun, lift and fetch. Any handlers on equal points further down the prizelist are separated in this way.

Once I have put down the points of a run on the judging sheet I will not change them and I never go back to look at them until the trial is over, so that it does not alter my concentration. It is very important to close one's mind to a dog's previous successes and concentrate solely on the run in hand.

Appendix: The First Trials

The history of sheep dog trials is like a partially-finished jigsaw – it is always nearing completion when another missing piece becomes evident. Other writers have documented well the fact that the honour of having the first-ever sheep dog trial in Britain went to Mr R. J. Lloyd-Price who organised the event at Gart Coch, the 'field of the red wild', about a mile from Bala in North Wales in October 1873. Many of us have made a pilgrimage to Bala and seen the site, both at the Centenary International Trials in 1973 and again when the International returned in 1980. Bala is always a cheery, hospitable place in which to sojourn with dog folk.

JAMES THOMSON

The bald statement that a Scot, James Thomson, with a small black and tan collie called Tweed, won that first trial in Britain is inadequate to cover the colourful background to the beginnings of one of the country's most popular pastimes. Mr Lloyd-Price himself, in an article on the trials in *Field* magazine of 18 October that year, faithfully reported every incident at the event which drew ten entries. He writes of one collie 'so diminutive a dog that he was produced from his master's pocket and held aloft to view his sheep'; one which 'fettered the sheep with his eye'; another whose sheep bolted into the river – this also happened at the 1980 International – and one whose charges became mixed up with a flock of geese.

There was always a missing piece in the jigsaw about Bala: who was, and what happened to James Thomson, whose only address in the *Field* report is 'Dumfriesshire'. I tried to fill in this piece of the puzzle in 1973, to coincide with the centenary trials, and completed the picture through finding a well-thumbed family Bible and a 98-year-old cheery soul who still had the Welsh tongue though far from the mountains where she used it as a child.

It was the missing chapter, so vital in that particular year when men who knew and worked sheep dogs sought to learn more of the man, born into a shepherding family in an outlying Dumfriesshire glen, later a packman heading south with his dogs and his goods, and now buried under Welsh soil in the churchyard of Pontfadog. I discovered first of all that James Thomson had come from Glenwhargen Farm in Scaur Water, not far from Penpont in Dumfriesshire – a 2,700-acre unit which has changed little since the days when the Thomson family herded there. The trail ended there for a while, so I managed to get a picture inserted in the *Scottish Farmer* with a request for any information about what

THE FIRST SHEEPDOG TRIAL TROPHY IN THE WORLD
WON BY JAMES THOMSON, AT RHIWLAS, WALES IN 1876
PRESENTED TO THE INTERNATIONAL SHEEPDOG SOCIETY BY HIS
WIDOW. JEAN THOMSON ON HER 102ND BIRTHDAY 1ST JUNE 1954

The first trial in Britain had this award for the winner, Scot Jimmy
Thomson.

happened to the Thomsons.

The puzzle was solved when I had a message from a well-known trials enthusiast, the late William Paul of Lochwinnoch, which took me to a place well removed from the runs of dog and sheep, a Paisley housing scheme, where I came across that Bible and James Thomson's daughter, Mrs Jonann Gilmour, then aged 98. Mrs Gilmour, the eldest of a family of seven daughters and one son born to the Thomsons in Wales, still remembered the tenanted farms of her father. She recalled Maes-y-Fallen near Bala where she was born; Bwlch in Harob-Llanfor parish; Cwy Cottage at Llandderfel; Cilnant in Glyn Traian parish and, last of all, Springhill farm, Glyn Traian which Thomson owned and where he died at the age of 65. They were all names on that Bible.

All of these farms were on the North Wales uplands where, at times, there were whole Scottish communities dotted along the mountains; where Jimmy Thomson would walk or take a pony and trap to trials and markets; and from where once he left for London to show Queen Victoria the worth of the working dog. All of this was a far cry from the burnside homestead of Glenwhargen, in Blackface and Cheviot country, where he was born in 1846 and which he left in 1870 taking the track with a pack on his back and dogs at his side. We must presume that he had been shepherding at Glenwhargen until about 1870.

On his travels selling cloth, wool and odds and ends he arrived at Bala and took on the running of a smallholding. In 1872 he came back to Dumfriesshire, married Jane Johnston from Drum Cottage, Durisdeer, and returned to Merioneth as a tenant on the estate of Mr R. J. Lloyd-Price of Rhiwlas. Lloyd-Price obviously spotted his tenant's skill with collies and in the following year on Gart Coch, he organised the trial which Jimmy Thomson won with Tweed.

'Tweed was a very common name with them all then', Mrs Gilmour, who lived with her daughter, Mrs Jean Pearston, told me. Her father 'always had at least two sheep dogs if not more and he had an awful lot of callers. I was brought up to speak Welsh and was very often called out if there was some business between him and Welsh farmers.' On one occasion during heated haggling over the price of a dog between Jimmy Thomson and a Welshman, the latter started into a tirade of Welsh. Called in to interpret, Mrs Gilmour told her father, 'He's swearing at you.' Promptly the Welshman was sent packing down the road.

Mrs Gilmour recalled, 'At these places where we lived, most of the farmers along the hills were Scottish. They were all quite happy among themselves.

'Father was always working with dogs and training them for trials. I remember him going away to some trials. A few were a good distance away. Sometimes he would go by pony and trap, but he did an awful lot of walking before we got a pony. He got many a prize at sheep dog trials. He sent a lot of dogs away and sometimes they came back on their own. Many times they must have swum across rivers to come home.'

Mrs Gilmour travelled to trials with her father near Bala. 'I remember there were some big turnouts. But father went all over to trials. He was also asked to go and arrange trials in different places, or to judge them, and he was away from home a lot. But he did an awful lot of work himself when he was at home, even although we had a manservant. I remember there were always dogs going about in the house. Mother did not object to them. Father was always quite happy in Wales but he said you had to keep your head and your eyes about you because they seemed to strike a hard bargain. He read a lot. He was always reading when he came in and had a minute or two to himself. It was either books or newspapers.'

Mrs Gilmour could still remember sheep shearing days and dippings at her father's farm. 'There would always be neighbours helping out. And it was nearly always Scotsmen who came, for there was this whole colony of them.' Her father, she recalled, was also a keen churchman. She could remember going to church at Pontfadog. She would attend the morning service, come out and go up the road where she had hidden something for her lunch, then return for the Sunday School. It meant being away from home from 10 a.m. until 4 p.m. She could also remember her father being a great letter-writer. Through sending dogs overseas, including some to the United States and Australia, there was always a good deal of correspondence.

After leaving Maes-y-Fallen and before taking ownership of Springhill farm near Oswestry in the early 1890s, Jimmy Thomson had other tenancies in North Wales. He was put out of one farm because he refused to vote (Liberal) for the landlord at an election. His story then ends at Springhill farm, and at Pontfadog churchyard where he is buried below the hillside.

EARLY SCOTTISH TRIALS

There are other parts in the jigsaw which sometimes appear to fit and sometimes seem to be the wrong shape. There is some uncertainty as to when the first trial in Scotland was held. A *Farming News* supplement of 1928 states that 'whatever its date may have been – it must have been in the early seventies' – the Carnwath trials undoubtedly hold the strongest claim to the title. The first prize was £1 and it was won by a young Pentland shepherd James Gardiner and a bitch named Sly. In 1975 the local Society ran a 'centenary' trial and that same year I found a grand-niece of Gardiner, Mrs Adam Murray of Braehead Village, Forth, Lanarkshire who presented the James Gardiner Centenary Cup.

However, the mystery deepened when the late John McIntyre, of Lochgilphead, sent me a clipping of an article written by the late ISDS Secretary James Reid in the *Scottish Field* of October 1951. Reid mentions a sporting magazine of 1876 in which a letter appeared from 'Arthur Cecil, Orchardmains, Innerleithen' in which the writer spoke of 'having had the management of some trials of the kind in Scotland'. Reid reports that two years after coming to Orchardmains, Cecil bought the winning bitch at the West Linton trials in 1876 for £10, then considered a high price for a working collie. Whether the trials which he 'managed' were trials which he and his brother had promoted at Orchardmains in 1876 – or earlier – or whether they were one of the three West Linton trials in 1874–1876, Cecil's letter did not say.

TRIALS IN
NEW ZEALAND

To throw another well-established piece of jigsaw out of the window, it is in fact doubtful if the first sheep dog trial was the one held at Bala, for it would appear that New Zealanders had organised one prior to that. In an article in the *New Zealand Farmer* in October 1977, Ian Sinclair mentions an excerpt from a book, *Early South Canterbury Runs* by Robert Pinney. It quotes from the *Timarua Herald* of February 3, 1869, the first account Sinclair had found of such a meeting: 'Trial of Sheep Dogs. The first of what is to be hoped will be an annual trial of sheep dogs took place on Friday last on Mr Fraser's run, Black Forest, Mackenzie Country. The conditions of the trial were to put three sheep into three separate pens in half an hour, the sheep having half a mile start.'

In correspondence with Mr Pinney, Ian Sinclair got a letter in reply which stated that in the *Oamaru Times* of July 9, 1869, there is an account of a dog trial at Wanaka on June 22–23 which was reported 'to be the third annual trial'. This then would place the first sheep dog trial as being held in 1866. Any advance on that?

Glossary

Bucht Sheep pen.

Brace (or doubles) The class at sheep dog trials where two collies are run together.

CEA Collie eye anomaly – a hereditary defect.

Classy Nice to look at and attractive while working.

Dew Claw A nail on the inside of the back leg which can cause problems if left to grow too long. Should be removed under veterinary supervision.

Eye The hypnotic power of collies to make stock move.

Flake A gate or obstacle on a trials course.

Flanking Movement of the dog to the back of the sheep either on the left or right-hand route, as commanded with the *come by* or *kwae tae me* orders.

Fluke Parasitic flat worms which infest animal livers, especially in sheep and cattle.

Folds, stells, rees Sheep pens or enclosures.

Gimmer A female sheep between its first and second shearings.

Gripping Allowing the dog to give the sheep a quick nip, mainly in the wool.

Heft A small geographical area of a hill sheep farm, possibly demarcated by a burn, hilltop, or hillend.

Hoggs Young sheep between weaning and their first shearing.

ISDS International Sheep Dog Society.

Lift The first stage of the fetching process, where the dog ends his outrun and begins to bring the sheep forwards.

Plain A dog with little style, inclined to carry his head too high.

Point of Balance The point at the back of the sheep where the dog must stop, when told, before bringing the sheep to the handler, in as straight a line as possible.

PRA Progressive retinal atrophy – a hereditary condition in which the nervous elements of the retina undergo progressive atrophy and the animal suffers from impaired vision in consequence.

Sciff To pass too close to the sheep.

Scope A dog with scope has a fast and wide outrun, with plenty of action.

Shedding Separating a group or individual sheep from the rest of the flock.

Stackyard A small enclosure originally used for building corn stacks.

Tup A ram.

Wearing Walking up to sheep and eyeing them.

Wethers Castrated male sheep.

Yeld A ewe which is not pregnant.

Bibliography

The following are titles of other books relevant to sheepdogs, training, trialling and the world of shepherding. All are published in Great Britain.

One Woman and Her Dog Billingham, Viv (Patrick Stephens Ltd, 1984)
The Shepherd's Wife Billingham, Viv (Patrick Stephens Ltd, 1986)
Sheepdogs, My Faithful Friends Halsall, Eric (Patrick Stephens Ltd, 1980)
Sheepdog Trials Halsall, Eric (Patrick Stephens Ltd, 1982)
The Farmer's Dog Holmes, John (Popular Dogs Publishing, 1960)
Sheepdogs at Work Iley, Tony (Dalesman Books, 1978)
The Sheep Dog – its Work and Training Longton, Tim and Hart, Edward (David and Charles, 1976)
The British Sheepdog Moorhouse, Sydney (H. F. and G. Witherby Ltd, 1950)
Country Diary Mundell, Matt (Gordon Wright Publishing, 1981)

Useful Addresses

International Sheep Dog Society
(Secretary – A. Philip Hendry)
Chesham House
47 Bromham Road
Bedford MK40 2AA

This is the governing body for the registration of border collies, and administrators and organisers of the National and International Sheep Dog Trials. Each of the home countries annually elects directors to the Society, and their newsletter contains a useful list of local trials being held during the season. They have world-wide membership and many affiliated trials and sheep dog organisations in this country and overseas.

Agricultural Training Board
32–34 Beckenham Road
Beckenham
Kent BR3 4PB

The Board has training officers based throughout the country, and local group members. They often organise courses for sheep dog training, where there is a demand.

Working Sheep Dog News
(Editor – Barbara Collins)
Ty'n-y-Caeau
Pwwlglas
Ruthin
Clwyd
North Wales LL15 2LT

A magazine which covers the trials world, with results and articles.

Border Collie Breeders Association
of America
Diane Whitehouse
Route 4
Box 157
Thackerry Road
McLeansboro
Illinois 62859

American Border Collie Newsletter
Casey Johnson
PO Box 596
King City
California 93930

American Border Collie Registry Inc.
(President – Dewey Jontz)
Runnells
Iowa 50237

American Border Collie Association
(Secretary – Mrs P. Rodger)
Route 4 Box 255
Perkinston
Mississippi 39573

Index

Index